Measure Up!

Yardsticks for Continuous Improvement

Richard L. Lynch
and
Kelvin F. Cross

Basil Blackwell

Copyright © Richard L. Lynch and Kelvin F. Cross 1991

First published 1991

First published in USA 1991

Basil Blackwell, Inc.
3 Cambridge Center
Cambridge, Massachusetts 02142, USA

Basil Blackwell Ltd
108 Cowley Road, Oxford, OX4 1JF, UK

Library of Congress Cataloging in Publication Data
Lynch, Richard L.
Measure Up! Yardsticks for Continuous
Improvement/Richard L. Lynch and Kelvin F. Cross.
p. cm.
'First published 1990'–T.p. verso.
Includes index.
ISBN 1–55786–099–8
1. Industrial productivity–United States.
2. Quality control–United States. 3. Business
logistics–United States.
4. Competition, International. 5. Performance
measurement. I. Cross, Kelvin F., 1953– II. Title.
HC110,152L96 1991
338'.06'0973–dc20   90–617 CIP

British Library Cataloguing in Publication Data
A CIP catalogue record for this book is available from the British Library.

Typeset in 11 on 13 pt Galliard
by Enset (Photosetting), Midsomer Norton, Bath, Avon
Printed in Great Britain by
T. J. Press Ltd, Padstow, Cornwall

Contents

$\diamondsuit$

$\blacklozenge$

Preface

◆

When we began developing the ideas for this book back in 1987, we knew that the yardsticks to measure productive performance at one company came up short. Real short. What we did not realize then was that the same problem was plaguing many firms around the globe.

We faced a specific problem: how to change the performance measurement system in one troubled firm to help it compete better. At about the same time, the Massachusetts Institute of Technology's Commission on Industrial Productivity was busy examining eight production industries ranging from older industries such as automobiles, steel, and textiles to newer ones including semiconductors, photocopiers, and computers. The researchers – 16 of MIT's top guns in the areas of economics, engineering, and science – came to a troubling conclusion: the United States is losing its dominant position in the world economy because of profound defects in the country's *private sector culture*, not because of unfair competition or ineffective government.

As part of the sweeping recommendations contained in *Made in America*, the Commission specifically recommended that industry develop techniques to *measure* and improve the efficiency and quality of the production process, and identify opportunities for progressive improvements in its performance. In particular, they called for new measures on three performance criteria: quality, cost, and delivery. We came to a similar conclusion back in 1987 when we identified quality, delivery, cycle time, and waste as the foundation for our measurement system.

The United States does not have a monopoly on outdated per-form-ance yardsticks and is not the only nation facing change. In Japan, studies have found that almost half of the executives surveyed were dissatisfied with their companies' measurement systems. In Europe, the Single European Act of 1987 will open the doors to a new wave of competition in 1992. Companies that operate in the European Community will have to compete on a more even playing-field – productivity must improve, customer retention must be earned, and companies will have to become more responsive to exploit new opportunities.

In response to these challenges, Harvard University sponsored a colloquium, 'Measuring Manufacturing Performance,' in January of 1989. The conference was a productive exchange of ideas between the academic world and practitioners from over 25 companies from around the globe. While much of the conference addressed what needed to be done, our suspicion that few, if any, companies were actually implementing new measurement systems was justified. Comments by the conference delegates reflected a consensus that quantum leap improvements were still needed if measurement systems were to help promote world-class competition. In particular, new systems would have to:

- focus on the customer
- forge tighter linkages between plant and local department measures
- be more dynamic, capable of changing when customer expectations or strategies change
- translate 'flexibility' into specific measurements
- link operations to financial results.

In short, the challenge raised at the Colloquium was to develop a radically new framework for performance measurement.

Measure Up! is our response to this challenge. We began the im-plementation process in a just-in-time production module in one plant of a multinational firm, expanded the concept throughout the order-fulfillment business system and finally applied our approach in new product introduction, and administration workflows as well. While we started innocently enough, we now realize changing per-formance measures attacks the corporate culture itself. The old yardsticks represent long-revered beliefs about management style, the workforce and the customer. As with any change, the old ways are defended and the new yardsticks resisted. Overcoming these obstacles is no easy task.

We tackled the problem head on. The approach in this book builds upon the principles of strategic planning, total quality control, activity accounting, just-in-time, and workflow simplification. Our contribution is that we have built on top of these world-class standards an innovative, performance-measurement system that consistently reinforces doing the right things, and doing them well.

◇

Acknowledgements

◆

While many people contributed directly and indirectly to this book, several key individuals helped shape our thinking and gave us the support and encouragement to complete this project.

First, we must thank Tom Vollmann and Jeff Miller from Boston University. Tom and Jeff have been strong proponents of cutting the 'Gordian knot' when it comes to performance measurement. The Manufacturing Roundtable conferences they invited us to participate in ('Implementing Manufacturing Strategies: Breaking Performance Measure Barriers' and 'The Manufacturing Executives' Forum on Performance Measurement') helped to solidify some of our ideas and expand others.

We must also thank Bob Kaplan and Robin Cooper from the Harvard Business School for their insights and feedback on our earlier drafts. C. J. McNair from the University of Rhode Island merits special thanks. It was C. J., with some prodding from Pat Romano of the National Association of Accountants, who helped us forge the linkage between the accounting system and operational controls. The section in chapter 10 on control systems could not have been written without her insight, energy, and friendship. Denis Lee from Suffolk University contributed greatly to our thinking in the areas of information systems and how to filter data and improve learning curves at the workcell level. We would also like to thank Arnold Judson, chairman of Gray–Judson–Howard, and Henry Foley, president and CEO of Gray–Judson–Howard. 'Jud' helped us put our program into a more strategic context and laid the foundation for our work on business operating systems in chapters 3 through 5. Henry's insights and experiences with service industries helped to put chapters 4 and 6 into focus.

The reader should not be left with the impression that we spent two years locked up in a room with consultants and professors. Our ideas could not have been formulated and implemented without the practitioners.

Most of our concepts were based on detailed observations, trial and error and successes at three companies. Each company was as different as night from day. One is a very successful manufacturer of high-performance integrated circuits. The second is a US *Fortune 500* computer manufacturer which underwent major restructuring in 1989. The third company is an international health and diet service company with over 10 million clients.

A valuable source of data came from industry practitioners. In the course of one year, we presented our approach to over 1,000 managers and individual contributors in ten cities across the US. The miles were worth it. Many of the concepts and refinements made to this book came about as the result of the suggestions or questions raised at these conferences.

Several 'practitioner' acknowledgements are also in order. Art Schneiderman, vice-president of quality and productivity improvement at Analog Devices Inc., stretched our targets when he shared with us his work on executive information systems, goal-setting, and quality improvement. In particular, his contribution on improvement 'half-life' was the foundation of our section on goals in chapter 8.

At Wang Laboratories, we thank Bob Aspell, Lou Pitocchelli, Alex Gliksberg, and Frank Walsh for their comments and contributions. There were also the dozens of change-makers in the factories and offices who actually implemented the program described in chapters 8 and 9. Without their help, our program might have been just another interesting idea.

At Weight Watchers International, a division of H. J. Heinz, Larry Appell made several contributions to our work on customer focus, mapping and information systems. Likewise we appreciate the contribution from Trevor Wheeldon of H. J. Heinz, UK.

From Hewlett-Packard (HP) we would like to thank Nancy Kerins of HP's medical division in Waltham, Massachusetts, and John Lemley from HP's microwave and communication group for sharing with us their thoughts on activity accounting and performance measures.

A special thanks goes to Steve Lynch and Steve Cosmopulos, of Cosmopulos, Crowley & Daly, Inc., for their suggestions to 'liven up' the book.

Finally, we extend our gratitude to our spouses and children for their encouragement, patience, and sacrifices.

December 31, 1989
Richard L. Lynch
Tyngsboro, Massachusetts
Kelvin F. Cross
Cambridge, Massachusetts

To: Patty, Marianne, Kevin, and Caren

When you can measure what you are speaking about, and express it in numbers, you know something about it; but when you cannot measure it, when you cannot express it in numbers, your knowledge is of a meagre and unsatisfactory kind . . .

William Thompson (Lord Kelvin), 1824–1907

1

◇

Do Your Yardsticks Measure Up?

◆

'What gets measured gets done' has never been so powerful a truth.

Tom Peters, *Thriving on Chaos*

Introduction

Most company performance yardsticks are too short, too rigid, or used more like a teacher's ruler – to whack rather than to motivate. The time is long overdue to replace these outdated yardsticks with a more dynamic measurement system; one that motivates continuous improvement in customer satisfaction, flexibility, and productivity – simultaneously. For many companies, improvement in these areas will be a matter of survival in the 1990s.

That is what this book is all about: measuring day-to-day operations to ensure top corporate performance. Throughout the book, we use the term 'performance measurement' in a specific context. It describes the feedback or information on activities with respect to meeting customer expectations and strategic objectives. In short, we are concerned with two simple questions:

- Are functions and departments doing the right things?
- Are they doing them well?

The purpose of performance measurement then is to motivate behavior leading to continuous improvement in customer satisfaction, flexibility, and productivity.

1

First-downs and touch-downs

In their book *American Business: A Two Minute Warning*, C. Jackson Grayson Jr and Clara O'Dell use the analogy of a sporting event to let us know that time is running out for American business.[1] Using American football as one example, the metaphor can be extended in terms of performance measurement in business.

The yardstick is clear. Ten yards is continuous improvement. The goal-line is the objective. The players on the field know exactly who their customers are. They see them in the stands and hear from them when they do not meet their fans' expectations. They are also keenly aware of the need to satisfy the owners, who have them under close scrutiny from the executive suite above the stadium. Football players are also aware of the strengths and weaknesses of their competition. The coaches have developed the game plan (usually a blend of the basics with some innovative or surprise plays), based on their scouting reports and knowledge of their team's advantages. The plays are set and it's time for kick-off.

As the game develops everbody pays attention to the measures. Foremost is how the team as a whole is executing the game plan. That is reflected in the score. The players also have their individual and group measures, depending on their specific role on the team: yards per carry for the running back (and the offensive line), percentage of passes complete for the quarterback, number of tackles for defensive linemen, and so on. Coaches have immediate feedback on the game plan. Critical plays are analyzed on instant replay to make real-time adjustments. The game goes on. Win or lose, the coaches and players know exactly what areas they need to improve.

How come the performance measurement systems in many *Fortune 1,000* companies are not this clear?

The answer is simple. Most measures throughout corporate America do not reflect the game plan. The ones that do are typically fragmented and isolated by functional specialty. For instance, quality measures are measured and reported by the quality department one week; cost measures are done by the finance department and reported another week; delivery measures are done by operations and reported daily. The result is that many of today's performance measures are promoting and rewarding behavior that hampers a company's overall performance.

Fumbling the ball

Consider the following examples, where top management depend on traditional performance measures to control their game plan, with disappointing outcomes.

A large electronics company pursues a strategy to become a flexible, low-cost producer. A just-in-time (JIT) strategy is developed outlining the basic changes required. Engineering reorganizes its production process to build one product at a time in continuous flow. Purchasing has its own game plan to help. Their old yardstick, purchase price variance, tells them how: lower purchase price. The buyers achieve their goals by buying in large quantities in the Far East and report progress against their cost objectives. Unfortunately, as lead times are lengthened by six weeks, manufacturing production requirements change. The apparent cost reductions in purchase cost are more than offset by rising inventory costs and the assembly lines wait idle for the material they need for actual orders.

A strategic objective in one company in a hi-tech industry is to become a highly profitable company by being a product leader. To measure the performance of its marketing and research and development (R&D) functions, the number of new products developed is the most watched performance barometer. An internal review, however, reveals that in a sample of 20 new product introductions, 80 percent missed the first customer ship date – most by well over a month. Also, the products are not fully documented for manufacturing. As a result, significant waste (engineering material changes, material cancellations, inventory) piles up in production. Nevertheless, R&D management cannot understand why manufacturing are unable to make shipments or why the accountant's ink is turning red. After all, their yardstick tells them they are developing new product at a record rate.

To increase market share, a computer service bureau embarks on a strategy to improve the timeliness of its voice mailbox service.

A program is implemented to accept verbal telephone orders to speed up order entry. The goal is to provide a new customer with service within 24 hours. At first, the new process appears to be successful by the on-time delivery measure; most new customers were on-line in a day. Later, an internal audit uncovers a 70 percent error rate in order entry caused by the new procedure. Some errors are caught by a manual, time-consuming reconciliation process. However, over 30 percent of customers continue to dispute their bills and refuse to pay. Many customers, frustrated with the administrative hassle, cancel the service and choose another vendor.

What do these examples tell us? Measurements in different functions did not consistently support the intended strategy. Activities that were cross-functional in nature were not evaluated that way. Furthermore, there was no linkage between the operational feedback and financial performance. Finally, the marketplace customer was ignored or only a partial set of his expectations were met.

Broken yardsticks

Peter Drucker, one of the foremost experts on management, has made two basic assertions about performance measurement. First, he maintains that few factors are as important to the performance of organization as measurement. Second, he laments the fact that measurement is the weakest area in management today!

Recent data back up Drucker's observation. In a survey sponsored by the National Association of Accountants and Computer Aided Manufacturing–International (CAM–I), 60 percent of the 260 financial officers and 64 operating executives in the US said they were dissatisfied with their performance measurement system.[2] Users were far more disappointed than preparers of the information. The study went on to say that 'this response clearly suggests the need to re-evaluate and revamp long standing performance measurement systems.' Even in Japan, 46 percent of executives believe their formal measurement systems leave something to be desired.[3]

If you are relying on traditional performance measures, you are probably not getting the answers you need to help you become more competitive. Even highly successful organizations have the sense of succeeding in spite of – rather than because of – performance measurements. For example, exhibit 1.1 shows that a group of managers from Hewlett-Packard's industry-leading medical products group had no trouble brainstorming on measurement problems and issues.

Exhibit 1.1 Measurement problems: Hewlett-Packard Medical Group

- too much emphasis on direct labor
- too much emphasis on accounting variances
- short-term financial mentality
- quality is not uniformly driven
- measures are not strategic
- measures promote local optimization
- poor cost feedback to design
- unclear link between short-term measures and long-term results
- each organization viewed separately
- measures fed up to top management are irrelevant

We have boiled down the various complaints and issues raised to us by hundreds of managers across a spectrum of manufacturing and service companies and found several common themes.

- Unless the yardsticks are specifically tuned to your game plan, they may be yielding either irrelevant or misleading information, or worse, provoke behavior that undermines the achievement of your strategic objectives.
- Measures that track each dimension of performance in isolation distort management's understanding of how effectively the organization as a whole is executing the game plan.
- Traditional yardsticks do not take into account the requirements and perspectives of customers (both internal and external).
- Bottom-line measures (such as profitability) come too late for mid-course corrections and remedial actions.
- Most yardsticks overlook key non-financial performance indicators.
- Yardsticks are often used liked a teacher's ruler in the classroom: for punishment rather than to promote learning.

- Like the yardsticks, many measurement systems are inflexible and limited in what they can do.

As noted earlier, even when established measures are aligned with the company strategy, reporting of performance information to management is fragmented. The result is mixed results on overall performance. For example, the quality department might report improvement in product acceptance, giving management a sense that things are improving. The finance department, on the other hand, might report separately the excess costs (scrap, rework, inventory, etc.) expended to improve quality. With this kind of feedback, trade-offs are hard to identify, let alone understand.

These failures led us to three conclusions about what a yardstick should do:

- Measures must *link operations to strategic goals*. Departments and functions should know how they are contributing separately and together in meeting their strategic mission.
- The system has to *integrate financial and non-financial information* in a way that is usable by operating managers. Also, management and employees need the right information at the right time to support decisions.
- The measurement system's real value would lie in its ability to *focus all business activities on customer requirements*.

Most managers we talked to never complained about getting too few reports! They generally get too many. Therefore we wanted to achieve our objectives while *reducing* the number of measurements and reports.

How to tailor measurements to your business

Many companies have come to the realization that they need to replace their yardsticks with something new. But what new tool? Leading experts say there are few pioneering examples and that you are basically 'on your own.'

This book addresses what needs to be done and suggests a process for how to do it. We have included many practical examples and tools for both manufacturers and service companies. In essence, it is both an executive primer for performance measurement system design and a practitioner's handbook on how to go about the change process in an individual department.

The bottom line is that the old yardsticks must go. We have replaced them with a more flexible measure, more a tape measure than a rigid rule, suggesting a more dynamic way to measure performance. The actual measurements, of course, must be custom tailored to suit your business.

If you need more convincing that your yardstick is not doing the job, chapter 2 summarizes the United States's tumultuous fall from industrial leadership and documents how traditional management practices such as managing by the numbers, reliance on technology, and the accounting model accelerated the fall. Some of the same lessons may hold true for Europe in 1992. Chapter 3 shows how measures can be both a catalyst for improvement and major means of sustaining strategic success. Key attributes of a strategic control system are introduced. Chapter 4 describes the process of taking a fresh look at your company through the eyes of your customer. The importance of mapping the workflows in your company's business operating systems is discussed. This step is a prerequisite to identifying critical success indicators.

A performance pyramid is constructed in chapter 5. It represents a new paradigm of performance. The model helps to promote organizational learning by relating actions to strategic objectives and encourages different functions to think and act more as a team. It also suggests a more balanced view of market and financial performance.

In chapter 6 both the performance and expectation dimensions of customer satisfaction are discussed. The objective for chapter 7 is to take a fresh look at productivity and see how performance tracks to the bottom line.

We put all these concepts together in chapter 8, taking you through the process of tailoring performance measures to suit your individual business. We do not pretend to be experts in your business. You are. But we have given you a tool that you can use to fit even 'one of a kind' situations. Chapter 9 covers implementation tactics. Finally, in chapter 10, we discuss how related systems such as the accounting model and compensation must be remodelled to provide a consistent, total performance measurement system.

For all you measurement pioneers about to begin the journey, use this book as your guide. We think it will 'measure up' to your expectations!

Summary

In an introductory fashion, this chapter explored many of the weaknesses of performance yardsticks. They are too short, too rigid, or used more like a teacher's ruler – to whack rather than to motivate. The new yardsticks must constitute a more dynamic measurement system; one that motivates continuous improvement in customer satisfaction, flexibility, and productivity – simultaneously. Specifically, performance measures must help managers and workers:

- measure what is important to their customers
- motivate operations to continually improve against customer expectations
- identify and eliminate waste – of both time and resources
- shift the focus of their organizations from bureaucratic, vertical empires to more responsive, horizontal business systems
- accelerate organizational learning and build a consensus for change when customer expectations shift or strategies call for the organization to behave differently.

Notes

1   C. Jackson Grayson Jr and Clara O'Dell, *American Business: A Two Minute Warning* (Free Press, New York, 1988).
2   Robert A. Howell, James D. Brown, Stephen R. Soucy and Allen H. Seed, *Management Accounting in the New Manufacturing Environment* (National Association of Accountants, Montvale, NJ, 1987).
3   Hideshi Nagamatsu and Tadao Tanaka, 'Management Accounting in the Advanced Manufacturing Surrounding – Comparative Study on Survey in Japan in the USA' (National Association of Accountants, Tokyo Affiliate, October 1988).

2

◇

Taking Off the Blinders

◆

Let them alone: they be the blind leaders of the blind. And if the blind lead the blind, both shall fall into the ditch.

Matthew 15:14

Innovative business people from around the globe are challenging traditional management tools and methods and questioning the old performance yardsticks. For example:

- JIT success stories are shattering conventional wisdom concerning lot sizes and inventory control.
- Vendor scheduling techniques are redefining the role of purchasing.
- Cross-functional teams such as 'Team Taurus' at Ford Motor Company are challenging the functional organization.
- Total quality control programs are exposing wasteful activities once considered a normal part of business.
- Activity accounting projects are bringing the accountant back into the factory and challenging traditional concepts of control.

These bold changes are confusing and unsettling to many managers. Under attack, managers blindly cling to their old beliefs. For example, while the decline of the US economy frustrates most American managers, it is only natural to turn to the methods that succeeded in the golden years of growth and innovation. Many business managers have adopted this strategy. The results, unfortunately, are rather like those of someone who keeps striking the same dead match.[1]

9

As the economic landscape is changing around the world, management must open their eyes to avoid falling into the ditch. In this chapter, we take a look backward at post-Second World War America, summarizing the storm that altered the landscape and changed forever the basis of competition. Next, we look ahead and examine the similarities to the present day as the countries of Europe prepare for a more even playing-field in 1992. Finally, we explore how traditional management beliefs helped forge many of today's performance yardsticks and how those yardsticks have hindered productive performance.

The storm that altered the American landscape

The tempest hit unexpectedly in the 1970s in the form of Japanese competition. It was devastating and hard to accept for many. Dreaming of those halcyon days following the Second World War will not restore America's standing as a major industrial power and the envy of the world. Good management and smart work will.

So how did America get caught napping?

The calm before the storm

American business enjoyed unprecedented prosperity following the Second World War. That prosperity was based on a set of unusual circumstances, as listed in exhibit 2.1. Pent-up demand for all types of durable and non-durable goods translated into a seller's market. Essentially, in a seller's market the customer may accept a high price or a long or erratic lead time for delivery of a standard product of marginal quality. In other words, the company can sell whatever it builds.

The short-term manufacturing strategy for American companies was simple: increase output. Nothing else mattered.

Isolated by distance and culture, American companies took a very parochial attitude towards business. After all, Europe and Japan were still recovering from the wreckage of the Second World War. America was the envy of the world. Everyone else had to play catch up.

Today, it is a different story. As former MIT president Paul E. Gray says: 'the corporate culture which developed over that time when we were king of the mountain doesn't serve us well now'.[2] In

---

Exhibit 2.1 The Five Pillars of US Industrial Might (following the Second World War)

1 The US market was eight times as large as the next biggest market. Industries enjoyed economies of scale unmatched anywhere else in the world.

2 America had the leading edge on technology, drawing on the talents of US scientists as well as European scientists who emigrated to America during and following the war.

3 America had the most highly skilled workers in the world. Huge investments made in public education and the GI bill put college within reach of many.

4 America was richer than other nations. Virtually all mass production commodities were introduced on US soil.

5 American managers were the 'cream of the crop.'

Source: Made in America: Regaining the Productive Edge, MIT Commission on Industrial Productivity (MIT Press, 1989).

---

fact, that kind of complacency is giving the mountain away. Just look around. Foreign competitors such as Honda are now producing as well as selling on American soil. For example, in 1978 Japanese automobiles were not made in the United States. Just ten years later, 695,020 Japanese cars rolled out of Japanese-managed assembly plants in America.[3]

The storm

The economic storm which hit hard in the 1970s had been brewing for many years. European and Japanese companies knew they were not number one and had to work hard just to catch up. They also had help from the US and their own governments in rebuilding their basic industries.

Just as the new factories sprang up, so did a new wave of managers. They faced a new world economy and developed the strategies to compete successfully in it. They also imported some of the best ideas from American business, universities and consultants. First came the work of Frederick Taylor (*Principles of Scientific Management*, published in 1911). Taylor's work was translated in Japan as *The Secret of Lost Motion* and sold over 2 million copies. A similar book on Taylor, *Secrets for Eliminating Futile Work and Increasing Productivity*, sold another million.[4] Although much maligned in the West today for separating planning from the work itself – leading to, as some contend, improved productivity at the expense of quality and human relations – his work was received in a far different spirit in Japan. In fact, Taylor's concept of minimizing wasted energy and resources is at the core of Japan's focus on continuous improvement (*kaizen*) and the elimination of waste (*muda*). Next came the work of Henry Ford (*Today and Tomorrow*, 1926). Taiichi Ohno freely credits Ford for his influence on the Toyota JIT system. Ohno was also influenced by the inventory system he observed in US supermarkets. These three sources helped to lay the foundation for JIT.

Also, following the Second World War, Dr Deming lectured extensively on the topic of statistical quality control. At the same time, Drs Juran and Armand Fiegenbaum lectured on the less statistical aspects of quality management company-wide.[5] Simple workflow improvement techniques and putting quality back in the hands of the workers provided a powerful competitive formula.

Early competition in the areas of textiles, steel, and consumer appliances went largely unheeded. American businessmen and consumers alike joked about cheap foreign products. Penetration of the wealthiest market had started. During this time, American companies not only ignored the competition, they got away from the basics and acquired totally unrelated businesses. For example, IT&T acquired a hotel chain and Mobil acquired Montgomery Ward. As Tom Peters says, companies were not 'sticking to their knitting.'

Market share began to erode first in the smokestack industries (e.g. textiles and steel) in the late 1960s, consumer appliances in the mid 1970s, automoblies in the early 1980s and electronics (microchips) in the mid 1980s.[6] America responded by erecting trade barriers such as tariffs, quotas, and domestic-content requirements. These have been largely ineffective and counterproductive. Furthermore, protectionist policy releases the pressure on American companies to improve their efficiencies and the consumer pays the price.[7]

Americans have already witnessed the impact of the storm. Some industries have been destroyed at the roots and markets have been turned upside down. Table 2.1 illustrates the extent of the damage.

Table 2.1 Erosion of US share of technology market

Technology	Pioneered by	US percentage of US market			
		1970	1975	1980	1987
Phonographs	US	90	40	30	1
Televisions					
Black and white	US	65	30	15	2
Color	US	90	80	60	10
Audiotape recorders	US	40	10	10	1
Videocassette recorders	US	10	10	1	1
Ball bearings	Germany	88	83	71	71
Machine tools					
Horizontal numerically					
controlled lathes	US	100*	92*	70	40
Machining centers	US	100*	97*	79	35
Telephone sets	US	99	95	88	25
Semiconductor manu-					
facturing equipment†	US	100	90	75	75
Cellular telephones	Scandinavia/				
	US	NA	NA	NA	40
Facsimile machines	US/Japan	NA	NA	NA	0

*estimates
†data for semiconductor merchant companies only. US company share includes production of foreign subsidiaries operating in US.
Source: reprinted courtesy of the *Boston Globe* and US Department of Commerce.

The wake of the storm

The storm has had a devastating effect on pillars of the American industrial empire. Exhibit 2.2 depicts the aftermath.

Storm warning: Europe 1992

The winds of change are blowing again, this time in Europe. Just as the Japanese competition is challenging American firms, the 12 nations of the European Community(EC) must brace themselves for heated competition in 1992.

The Single European Act of 1987 calls for a 'single market' in Europe starting in the year 1992. Exhibit 2.3 depicts some of the barriers and opportunities facing Europe today.

Exhibit 2.2 The Erosion of the Five Pillars (competing the 1980s and 1990s)

1 The US market is no longer eight times as large as the next biggest market. Japan is half as large and Europe in 1992 will be larger.

2 The US is no longer the technology leader in many industries and is on the verge of losing the race in emerging industries such as high-density TVs and custom chips.

3 America no longer has the most highly skilled or best educated workers. The US has lagged behind Canada, France, West Germany, Italy and Japan in productivity in the 1960s and 1970s.

4 US citizens have many peers today in terms of purchasing power.

5 As far as management ability, the 'crop' is getting creamed.

Source: Made in America: Regaining the Productive Edge, MIT Commission on Industrial Productivity (MIT Press, 1989).

Exhibit 2.3   Single market in Europe

Barriers before 1992

- Different standards: product regulations, safety, health and environmental, consumer protection
- Preoccupation with nationalism and protectionism by both governments and business lobbyists
- Restrictive public procurement policies
- Special tax advantages for local firms

Opportunities after 1992

- Europe is the second largest economic block behind North America with a population of 323 million
- More competitive environment (even playing-field)
- Consumers will be given more choice
- Prices will drop as a result of increased competition

Source: James W. Dudley, *1992: Strategies for the Single Market* (Kogan Page, London, 1989).

Just as American managers held on to outdated management practices, many European managers have operated in a distorted
marketplace. Customers had less choice and paid extra costs to cover
various regulations. Workflows were encumbered with unnecessary
steps and procedures to meet varying standards. One fact the managers in the single market must come to terms with is that more
opportunity will certainly mean more competition from within the
EC and outside it. As one European strategic management consultants puts it:

The European Commission's attitude to competition is wholly inward in its
approach. It supposes that by creating internal competition companies will
become leaner and fitter to contest external competition. Yet it ignores the
fact that many global Japanese and North American organizations are
already strongly competitive and they become the major beneficiaries in the
Single Market.[8]

As companies scramble to adjust to changing customer profiles, vast
improvements in quality and service, new supplier–customer
relationships and productivity pressures, new performance
yardsticks will be needed to see how firms measure up in 1992.

False idols

Yardsticks are symbolic of management beliefs and culture. They are
used in good faith and will not be easily replaced. However, in order
to change the yardsticks, the shortcomings of traditional management practices, including management by objectives (MBO), throwing money and/or technology at problems, and the accounting
model, must be exposed.

Belief in 'the system'

As noted earlier, in a seller's market all that counts is output. The only
yardstick that matters is 'making the numbers.' Large bureaucracies
are created to meet the task and the finance department enjoys a
strong power base. In the US, for example, increased emphasis on
external reporting brought about by the Securities Exchange
Commission (SEC), the Financial Accounting Standards Board
(FASB), and generally accepted accounting principles requirements
also raised the status and changed the focus of the accountant. In fact,

until recently the top American university/business school graduates were specialists in finance, auditing, accounting, and tax law, not operations management or management accounting.

20–400 vision

It has been well documented that the obsession with quarterly financial results has hampered long-term competitiveness in the US.[9] Business sector capital investment has been lower in the US than in Japan or West Germany, as has spending in R&D.[10] The short-term focus can best be seen in a comparison of Japanese- and American-managed companies. US managers put return on investment and share-price increase as their top objectives, with everything else a distant second; whereas Japanese managers ranked market share, return on investment, and ratio of new products as being of equal importance.[11] The focus on short-term financial results filters down through the company ranks. Financial numbers often dominate 'operational reviews' at the group, division, and department level. Investment in equipment necessary for long-term competitiveness is often rejected in favor of projects with quick (often temporary) paybacks. Making the numbers sometimes means shipping a project 'before its time'.

Specialists at fragmentation

During the postwar years, Western managers turned increasingly to functional organizations under the guise of optimization and cost control. Until then, most companies were modeled after the Du Pont 'divisionalized structure.' Each (smaller) division had all the functions necessary to do business: R&D, engineering, purchasing, production, distribution, and sales. With a change towards more centralization, new functional organizations emerged. The wisdom at the time was that centralization promoted efficiencies. It was easier to manage and control costs if all engineers reported to one organization, all manufacturing specialists to another, and so on.[12] While certain economies of scale were realized, this kind of organization caused two significant problems:

1 Company employees were insulated from other departments within the same company.
2 The distance between the employee and the customer was increased.

A closely related problem to meeting the numbers was the understanding of control. Again it was a numbers game: beat your budget. The fragmentation of operations was reinforced by the budget process and rewarded by the performance appraisal system.

Management by whose objectives?

Perhaps the biggest culprit in the management malaise of many traditional companies has been management by objectives, or MBO.

MBO, as commonly applied in organizations, is a process in which manager and subordinate sit down at the beginning of each performance period and agree upon individual job goals which subsequently serve as a basis for personal performance assessment.[13] Proponents of MBO say that it is a system for managing an organization: holding managers accountable; encouraging all employees to contribute to department goals; coordinating goals within the organization; and measuring results.[14]

Even the proponents of MBO recognize its shortcomings: a significant portion of the courses they offer is typically devoted to solving the problems caused by MBO.

What are those problems?

First, MBO foster competition rather than teamwork because it is a mechanism for assessing *individual contributions* at review time.

Second, in MBO goals are set by senior management that may or may not be strategy-related. MBO goals often ignore the customer and are based on past performance.

A third major problem is that MBO centers on the manager–subordinate relationship within the department's vertical structure, rather than on the horizontal workflow independent of organizational boundaries.

Fourth, MBO objectives once set, tend to become fixed throughout the organization. Adapting to changes in the external environment is often difficult.

Finally, MBO measures themselves tend to be one-dimensional, often financially oriented.

As one consultant, familiar with both European and American styles of management, put it: 'There is still great resistance within the United States to any management style other than a hierarchical system, where the employers make all the major decisions because they have all the answers.'[15]

In short, well-intentioned MBO objectives have tended to isolate and fragment the information companies need to become more competitive.

Technology's broken promises

For far too long American management have relied on 'technology to the rescue.' Lately, however, investments in technology have resulted in broken promises. For example:

- Harley-Davidson invested in miles of automated material-handling equipment, only to derail them after they implemented a JIT approach.
- General Electric gambled on the factory of the future and lost $120 million.
- IBM built a highly automated plant in Lexington, Kentucky. The Proprinter built there has 60 percent fewer parts than its predecessor. It could be snapped together by an individual assembler in 3½ minutes, making the expensive plant a bit of overkill.

Broken promises also come in smaller packages.

One hi-tech company invested heavily in state-of-the-art computer-aided design (CAD) systems dedicated for its designers. The CAD database consisting of all part numbers and their specifications allowed designers to perform certain tasks quicker. By all existing measures, productivity per designer improved significantly. The new CAD systems, however, were implemented without adequate evaluation of how downstream users of the data would be affected. As a result, fabrication, assembly, and test each maintained their own database. Having several databases, each with different information for the same part number, led to duplication of effort, product information errors, and delays in new product introduction.

A production department justified a new automatic insertion machine on the basis of number of insertions per minute capability. Analysts had no trouble showing senior management a fast payback. On the shopfloor, the machine was as fast as promised. The only problem was that the downstream operation could only process a fraction of the new machine's output and work-in-process buried the highly touted cost savings.

What do these examples suggest? Management often grab at the technology solution when the problem has not been fully understood. Sometimes investments in technology fail because they are misapplied or are not fully supported. At other times the engineer's fascination with the 'bells and whistles' leads to more complex systems than are necessary. Delicate systems are more prone to failure. Flexible manufacturing systems are a good example. Are they really a production advance or the factory version of the Concorde?[16]

These lessons demonstrate the wisdom behind the slogan: simplify, integrate, then automate. Throwing money or technology at a problem is not always the answer. The New United Motor Manufacturing Inc., or NUMMI (a joint venture between General Motors and Toyota), located in Fremont, California, is a case in point.

High quality Novas and Geos that are made at NUMMI cost $1,000 less to produce than comparable domestic models. These cars come out of the same plant (and most of the same workers) that was shut down in 1982 after years of strikes, high absenteeism, shoddy workmanship and rampant drug abuse. What changed? *It wasn't massive investments in new technology.* In fact, a visitor in the 3 million square foot facility is more impressed at NUMMI as a human oriented rather than a high tech operation. True, robots are visible in the body and paint shop and lift the heavy stuff. But mostly it's the workers who are visible, wielding screw guns and tooling along on bicycles carrying needed parts. What changed was management's philosophy about work and the workers.[17]

The accountant's distorted prism

Many of today's management accounting systems are under fire for not providing relevent feedback for operational control and generating misleading product cost data. The problem is not that accountants prefer red. They have been viewing operations through a foggy lens.

Many of the current accounting problems arise from outdated standard costing systems. Designed primarily to satisfy external financial reporting purposes, they simply have not kept pace with changes in the manufacturing environment. Just as a prism has three sides to view a continuous spectrum, the accounting model casts three glimpses of operational activities: investment justification, product cost, and performance measurement.

Investment justification

The wrong yardstick is often used when making investment decisions. The basic flaw is not the short return demanded on investment. Fast paybacks are necessary today, given the short lifecycle of many products. The problem lies in how and where the information is captured.

First, typical projects are put together from a local viewpoint and the impact on the local operation or function is evaluated. Seldom are downstream or upstream concerns discussed at company 'capital review committees.'

The second problem lies in what makes up the project benefits. The finance department typically assists the operations manager in the form of discounted cash-flow analysis. Cost savings in terms of labor and space are usually detailed and quantified. Great care is taken with the accuracy of the numbers: payback in 11.24623 months. Little attention is given to the so-called non-quantifiables, such as quality, cycle time, and delivery. Yet these variables make or break a firm's competitive edge.

The bottom line is that the short-term focus on local productivity (i.e. labor savings) has produced a competitive backlash. Incremental investments made typically do not live up to expectations. Investments in longer-term projects of strategic importance are postponed or killed.

Product cost

For years, most companies never thought much about their product cost model. The calculation was routine:

product cost = direct materials + direct labor + overhead

where overhead was allocated to product based on direct labor. This model worked very well in an environment where products were homogeneous and direct labor and materials were easily traceable to the product. Overhead was not a significant factor and was simply allocated on an 'average' overhead (i.e. volume) basis to all products.

However, as direct labor shrunk over the 1970s and 1980s, overhead rates soared – as did the number of products offered. Many companies reported overhead rates in the 600–1,000 percent range! Furthermore, increased competition from abroad and new start-ups put additional pressure on profit margins. Operating managers turned increasingly to the accountant for information:

- What product lines were making money?
- What product lines were losing money?
- Do some products require more overhead than others?

Increasingly, the accountant was unable to answer these important questions based on the data that the traditional standard cost model was generating.

Groups such as Computer Aided Manufacturing–International, or CAM–I (a consortium of government, industry, accounting firms, and universities in the US), the National Association of Accountants, university professors, and consultants have documented the shortcomings of the cost model. Exhibit 2.4 lists some of them.

In short, in many firms the product cost model has obscured important cost information by misreading activities and providing erroneous product cost data. Making decisions on this information alone has led to companies dropping profitable products and continuing with losers, plant reductions, and increased outsourcing.

Exhibit 2.4 Shortcomings of traditional approaches

- pricing errors
- improper make versus buy decisions
- irrelevant and untimely variance analysis
- misallocation of capital and resources
- non-productive, expensive vouchering
- misidentification of cause and effect relationships
- improper design incentives

Source: John T. Lemley, Hewlett-Packard, presented at the 'Cost Management Solutions' conference, sponsored by the Manufacturing Institute, Atlanta, 1989.

Performance measurement

Management accounting systems' treatment of performance measurement has also been roundly criticized.[18] The basic argument is that the traditional 'accounting model' which equates labor productivity and full utilization of equipment with successful performance misses the point. Measures used for inventory valuation and external financial reporting are counterproductive when also used to guide and measure business performance. Many consultants, academics, and professionals have joined the crusade against the use of such traditional performance measures as utilization, labor efficiencies, and material variances, for controlling operations in the new manufacturing environment.

The same accounting model neglects to treat performance outside of manufacturing. As a result few measures other than aggregate selling and general administration cost and budget variance have much attention paid to them.

Several outspoken critics put the accounting model squarely on the line. Robert S. Kaplan of the Harvard Business School puts it this way:

Accounting and financial executives must redirect their energies – and their thinking – from external reporting to the more effective management of their companies' tangible and intangible assets. Internal management accounting systems need renovation.[19]

Management consultants Robert A. Howell and Stephen R. Soucy agree:

Today, the focus of manufacturing has changed. Yet, many accounting departments have not updated their control mechanisms and processes. Operating controls need to reflect the concern of new manufacturers.[20]

Perhaps the most comprehensive trashing of traditional performance measures came from the CAM–I group in its seminal work, *Cost Management for Today's Advanced Manufacturing*. They concluded that existing measurement systems are ineffective barometers of world-class performance because they do not isolate non-value-added costs, do not penalize overproduction, and inadequately quantify non-financial performance indicators such as quality, throughput, and flexibility. Table 2.2 shows the folly of some traditional measures.

Table 2.2 Traditional measures that inhibit world-class performance

Measurement	Action	Result
Purchase price	Purchasing increases order quantity to get lower price, ignoring quality and delivery	Excess inventory; increased carrying costs; supplier with best quality and delivery may be overlooked
Machine utilization	Supervisor runs the machine in excess of daily unit requirement to maximize machine utilization	Excess inventory; wrong inventory
Set-up in standards	Encourages high run quantity	Excess inventory
Scrap factor built into standard cost	Supervisor takes no action if no variance	Inflated standard; minimum scrap threshold built in
Standard cost overhead absorption	Supervisor overproduces work-in-progress to get overhead absorption in excess of expenses	Excess inventory
Indirect/direct headcount ratio	Management, not total cost, controls the ratio	Indirect labor standards wrongly established; total cost not in control
Scrap dollars	Scrap dollars drive corrective action priority	Direct-level impact on flow hidden in dollars
Cost center reporting	Management focus is on cost centers, not activities	Opportunities to reduce costs are missed when common activities are overlooked
Labor reporting	Management focus is on direct labor, which is fixed and relatively small, instead of an overhead, which is variable and large	Missed cost-reduction opportunities; major overhead activities not exposed
Earned labor dollars	Supervisor maximizes earned labor, keeps workers busy	Excess inventory, schedule attainment gets lower priority; emphasizes output
Overhead rate	Management, not total cost, controls rate	Overhead levels improperly established; high-cost activities hidden

Source: Tom Pryor, Motorola, Inc.

The CAM–I group made five basic recommendations to improve performance reporting:

1 Develop a hierarchical measurement system that links business, plant, and shopfloor performance.
2 Identify and quantify the company's cost/performance drivers.
3 Identify non-value-added activities.
4 Eliminate inhibiting measures.
5 Simplify processes to minimize or eliminate non-value-added activities.

The accounting model is quickly losing its revered position in the corporate halls, having generated misleading product cost data, failed to provide strategic information on new investments, and provided irrelevant or dysfunctional feedback on activities.

Summary

In order to start building a new performance measurement system in your company, the following key points must be accepted by management.

- Firms are losing competitive ground because of fundamental flaws in management philosophy and practice, including the *use of performance measures*.
- Companies must place added emphasis on market share and new product introduction *measures* and less emphasis on short-term financial results.
- MBO-oriented companies must question question how *objectives and measures* are established and communicated.
- Specialization by function has led to isolation and fiefdoms in many companies and has increased the distance between employees and the customer. As a result, *performance information* is fragmented and *measures* important to the customer are lost.
- Technology alone will not save the day. Management must re-think the role technology plays in today's business environment and *measure its impact* on customer satisfaction, flexibility, and productivity.
- The accounting model must be updated to reflect activities. Specifically, it must provide *strategic information* on product cost and investments, and *feedback* on operational activities.

These issues must be understood and a commitment made to change. Otherwise, management policies, reward systems, and accounting controls will prove to be insurmountable obstacles in building a world-class performance measurement system.

Notes

1 MIT Commission on Industrial Productivity, *Made in America: Regaining the Productive Edge* (MIT Press, Cambridge, Mass., 1989).
2 Charles A. Rodin, 'America is Ailing at its Corporate Core,' *Boston Globe*, May 3, 1989.
3 'Then & Now,' *Inc.*, tenth anniversary issue, June 1989.
4 Charles J. McMillan, *The Japanese Industrial System* (Walter de Gruyter, New York, 1984).
5 David A. Garvin, *Managing Quality* (Free Press, New York, 1988).
6 Eliyahu M. Goldratt and Robert E. Fox, *The Race – for a Competitive Edge* (Creative Output, Milford, Conn., 1986).
7 *Made in America*.
8 James W. Dudley, *1992: Strategies for the Single Market* (Kogan Page, London, 1989).
9 *Made in America*.
10 H. Thomas Johnson and Robert S. Kaplan, *Relevance Lost: The Rise and Fall of Management Accounting* (HBS Press, Cambridge, Mass., 1987).
11 J. C. Abegglen and George Stalk Jr, *Kaisha: The Japanese Corporation* (Basic Books, New York, 1985).
12 Tom Peters, *Thriving on Chaos* (Harper & Row, New York, 1987).
13 George S. Ordiorne, *MBO II: A System of Managerial Leadership for the '80s* (Fearon Pitman Publishers, Belmont, Cal., 1987).
14 Dale D. McConkey, *How to Manage by Results* (AMACOM, American Management Association, New York, 1983).
15 Guy Halverson, 'Swedes Better than Japanese?,' *Boston Globe*, 1989.
16 Harley Shaiken, *Work Transformed* (Holt, Rinehart & Winston, New York, 1984).
17 Daniel Forbes, 'The Lessons of NUMMI,' *Business Month*, June 1987.
18 There are several exhaustive studies describing the problem. A few good ones are: Robert A. Howell, James D. Brown, Stephen R. Soucy, and Allen H. Seed, *Management Accounting in the New Manufacturing Environment*, Bold Step Series (National Association of Accountants, Montvale, NJ., 1987); Johnson and Kaplan, *Relevance Lost: The Rise and Fall of Management Accounting*; C. J. McNair, William Mosconi, and Thomas Norris, *Meeting the Technology Challenge: Cost*

Accounting in a JIT Environment, Bold Step Series (National Association of Accountants, Montvale, NJ, 1988).

19 R. S. Kaplan, 'Yesterday's Accounting Undermines Production', *Harvard Business Review,* July–August 1984.

20 B. Howell and S. R. Soucy, 'Operating Controls in the New Manufacturing Environment,' *Management Accounting,* October 1987.

3

◇

Dynamic Strategies Need Dynamic Yardsticks

◆

In strategy it is important to see distant things as if they were close and to take a distanced view of close things.

Miyamoto Musashi, Kendo Master, 1645

Wasn't strategic planning the answer to the management malaise in the 1970s? If so, why have investments in strategic planning let so many companies down? Part of the reason is that all too often companies set a new course but forget to take along a compass. Missing in many strategic plans is performance feedback on three important questions:

1 As business strategies are implemented, are operating managers focusing on the right issues and priorities?
2 How well is the company as a whole doing in implementing the strategies?
3 When and how should strategies be redirected?

Strategic planning is a process which documents a set of choices made by management of a business describing the mission, objectives, goals, strategies, and supporting action plans along with the rationale and implications associated with these choices. The choices relate to the scope of an organization's products/services, markets, key capabilities, growth, return, and allocation of resources.

The focus of the strategic plan is primarily external to the firm – on its industry, competitors, markets, and customers. The time horizon is typically about five years. For example, many companies are re-structuring and developing new strategies to compete in the single market in Europe in the 1990s.

Several outstanding texts have already been written about the strategy development process.[1] How to develop a strategic plan is beyond the scope of this book. Our purpose is to show how measures are tied to the strategy and to develop the framework for a strategic control system.

Assessing your competitive position

Most strategic plans begin with an assessment of the firm or organ-ization as a starting-point. Both the external and internal environ-ments come under close scrutiny.

External environment

Customer needs

Who are your customers? What are your customers looking for today and how are you satisfying their needs? What business/markets are you in and will these change in the future? What effect will these changes have on your market, the way you do business, and the way your company is structured?

Technological advances

What is the technology in the industry today and how is it changing? What new technologies will your company get into or need to get into in the future and how will this affect your market and the way you do business?

Competition

Who are your competitors? How is your company positioned and perceived in the marketplace? What are your competitors doing, where are they going and how do you need to react to their changes? Will there be additional competition in your marketplace in the future? Are you getting into new product markets and who are your competitors in these new markets? What are your strategies for competing against these competitors?

Internal environment

X *Product plans*

(Includes product line strategies and individual product plans.) Where are your products in the lifecycle of existing products? What products are being phased out and what new products are being phased in? What new product markets are you getting into and what are your plans for these products?

X *Strategic project plans*

What strategic projects are in existence or planned? What will be the impact across multiple organizations?

Operational project plans

X What operational plans (internal to the organization) are in place or planned?

X *Capacity plan*

How is your capacity being utilized in the current environment? How is your company adapting to change in business activities?

X **Charting a strategic course**

The next step in developing the strategic plan is understanding where the gaps are between the current setting and the ideal position. Companies typically analyze their strengths, weaknesses, threats, opportunities, risks, and dependencies.

X *Strengths*

What does your company currently do well: products, systems, procedures, activities, or functions? These should be reinforced and/or built upon.

Weaknesses

What doesn't your company do well: products, systems, procedures, activities, or functions? How can they be corrected?

Threats

The activities, environmental factors, or inefficiencies that could prevent you from achieving your goals. These must be sought out and eliminated.

Opportunities

Is there any unique or new activity that could allow you to move in a new direction, exploit and develop your strengths, or overcome your weaknesses?

Risks

An assessment of the threats and the consequences of failure and the establishment of risk management programs.

Dependencies

What support do you need from other organizations or functions to correct weaknesses, minimize your threats and risks, and exploit your opportunities?

The gaps identified form the basis for setting strategic objectives and prioritize the action plans.

A call to action

The rubber meets the road when strategic objectives are developed. Strategic objectives are stated in terms of actions/changes required of the organization in *measurable* terms, for example:

- faster time-to-market
- triple inventory turns
- 2–4-week manufacturing cycle time

- cut waste by 50 percent
- 100 percent on-time deliveries.

Arnold Judson, in his book *Making Strategy Happen: Transforming Plans Into Reality*, states that the more effectively management addresses five key issues, the more successful it will be in achieving substantial and lasting changes in how the organization works.

1. How thoroughly does everyone affected by or involved in carrying out the strategy understand the following?
   - What are the needs of their customers.
   - What is to be achieved and why.
   - How the strategy is to be accomplished, and to what timetable.
   - What resources will be applied.
   - What specific changes in behavior are required of each person involved.
2. How strong is the commitment of relevant managers and employees to implementing the strategy successfully?
   - How credible do they find the objectives and strategy?
   - To what extent do they 'own' the objectives and strategy?
   - To what extent have they participated directly in analyzing options and formulating the strategy?
3. How completely have the resources required to implement the strategy been identified and provided (including funds, tools, skills, and time)?
4. How systematic a process has been instituted for tracking implementation progress and for making mid-course corrections?
   - What gains are projected and how will these be measured and monitored?
   - How will actual experience be matched against forecasted results, and how will timely revisions be made in the implementation plan to reflect developing experience?
5. How consistent and credible a climate of accountability is maintained throughout the implementation period?
   - How strongly do those who have made commitments believe they must make good their promises?
   - What are the consequences when the groups and individuals succeed or fail; how congruent are rewards with success?
   - How visible and consistent are performance measures?

When a strategic plan is formulated using a participative process involving those managers in the entire organization who are essential for strategy implementation, issues 1–3 can be effectively resolved. The resolution of issues 4 and 5 depends on the effectiveness of leadership behavior and the appropriateness of the measurement system.

Dynamics of strategy implementation

Before discussing how operations must be linked to top business strategy, it is important to understand the dynamics of strategy implementation in greater depth. The causes of failures in implementation are more subtle and numerous than poor follow-through. These causes stem from the fact that almost every strategic plan calls for major changes in how organizations work. The successful achievement of these changes requires durable and far-reaching changes both in how the organization works *as a total system* and *how individual departments and people behave* in that system.

Demands on the organization

Most strategies aim to improve business performance – faster growth, more share of market, better returns, higher profits, etc. Typically such strategies call for an organization to operate differently. For example, one strategy may require new products and services that better meet customers' needs to be brought to market in half the customary time. Another strategy aimed at improving customer satisfaction may require substantial improvements in product and service quality. A third strategy may press for more aggressive pricing, enabled by greatly reduced costs.

Successful implementation of such strategies often requires fundamental changes in the behavior of an existing organization and its operating systems. This includes all the functions, people, technology, workflows, policies and procedures, and institutional systems (e.g. planning, information (including performance measures), control, rewards, communications) and the way these interact to carry on an existing business. Each organization has its own culture and performance capabilities (strong and weak), including an inherent ability to resist change.

As practitioners everywhere know, the elements within an organization interrelate in extraordinarily complex and subtle ways. It is difficult to anticipate accurately how any changes required by a business strategy will impact the business. But some companies do it better than others.

Typically, in a strategic plan, the changes required of an organization to implement a particular strategy are outlined in the form of a sequence of action steps. Each action step specifies the scope of work to be done, the nature of the 'deliverable,' the resources required including the key individuals who will be working on the task, the person accountable for meeting the commitment, and the date of completion. Implementation of an action plan (and by implication, the strategy) is monitored and measured by relating actual progress against the completion of the tasks in the action plan.

But completing an action plan does not necessarily mean that the strategy has been successfully implemented. Achieving an action usually marks only the start of a change in the business system. Fully realizing the intent of that change by making it operational over a sustained period of time is another matter. For example, a plan's action steps might call for the installation of workcells in a manufacturing process, the development of new skills, or the design of a new product introduction process. Once these actions have been achieved, a monitoring procedure based only on the plan itself would signal that implementation was complete. Yet, in actuality, the gains intended by such actions would not be realized until a subsequent consistent change in operations had been achieved over time.

Feet of clay

While short-term gains are often ballyhooed at the end of a pilot project, they sometimes have fatal weaknesses for the long haul. Consider the following case.

A large electronics firm experimented with a JIT workcell approach to reduce throughput time and improve quality and worker morale. The results of the pilot project were striking. Gone were the mountains of work-in-process, together with the material systems to move it and the tracking slips to control it. In their place were independent work teams capable of assembling and testing complete products. Over time, however, management changes, inadequate training, and no visible performance measurement system geared to the JIT strategy, led to performance decline. An audit of the production area showed throughput time and inventory levels on the rise, incomplete kits being issued regularly and a return to batch processing and quality control inspection.

This example is not unusual. Even Eliyahu Goldratt's and Jeff Cox's widely acclaimed *The Goal* (North River Press, 1984) revealed the plant portrayed in the story had feet of clay. Goldratt's revised 1986 edition contains an epilogue in which the plant manager, Alex Rogo, reveals that *The Goal* was a story about failure, not success. Yes, the plant changed, performance improved dramatically, and the threat of closure went away. However, in the new epilogue, Alex recounts to a friend how, after the initial jump, performance stabilized and then began to deteriorate, and the plant became more and more resistant to change.

Ways of sustaining focus

Full implementation of a strategy requires the completion of two phases:

1) The initial *installation* of changes to the business system, as specified by actions in the plan.
2) Making these installations *operational* over time.

The means available to any senior executive to sustain long-term momentum and organizational focus on the strategy typically include the following.

- *A solid plan* – the detailed outline in the strategic and/or operating plan describing the work to be completed in order to achieve the installation of the initial changes in each business system. The more explicit and comprehensive this action detailing, the better the road map available to everyone concerned in assigning tasks, determining resources required, drawing up timetables and setting out accountabilities. Such a road map can be used as a primary tool for monitoring and tracking implementation progress.

- *Leadership* – the personal behavior of the most senior executive accountable for strategy implementation. Especially important is behavior that conveys the leader's attention and concern in following implementation progress, along with the application of rewards, recognition, and penalties.
- *Controlled experiments* – the achievement of highly visible early 'successes' that can be attributed to carrying out the strategy. Such implementation outcomes, if widely perceived as beneficial, can reassure everyone concerned that the organization is on the right track and that the strategy is 'paying off.'

Two major dilemmas often undermine successful strategy implementation. First, top-level executives, along with their direct reports, no matter how competent and well intentioned, cannot be relied upon consistently to devote the time and attention required to drive strategy implementation at the working level over a 2–3-year period.

The other dilemma stems from the fundamental difference between the nature of the business strategy and day-to-day operations. Business strategy is integrated and systemic. It places performance demands on the organization as a whole and the individual departments. But day-to-day activities are often fragmented by functional specialty. How then can an integrated effort be mobilized to achieve strategic objectives when the attention of most people is focused on parochial priorities and local agendas?

Operational acceptance

Even when there is a strong, widely shared commitment to carry out a strategy, these good intentions quickly fade and implementation breaks down as normal day-to-day pressures and crises cause individuals to shift their priorities and diffuse their efforts. What starts out as an attempt to carry out a particular set of actions to implement a strategy soon degenerates into 'business as usual.' Only some actions get installed and those that are apparently 'complete' never see full realization in the operational phase.

Typically department measures tend to reflect the department manager's view of what constitutes excellence in performance. Unfortunately, this may or may not be relevant to what constitutes excellence in the performance of the entire system of which that department is a single component. For instance, cutting cost in one department may create more costs in another department.

The process of change where measures drive actions

In our opinion, performance measurement is the most powerful single means to ensure implementation success. Properly designed and implemented performance measures continue to motivate groups long after the initial attention wears off; long after managers have come and gone and long after workers can recite the new strategy.

When measures are customer-driven, strategically aligned and integrated, and instituted at the business unit, division, and department levels, they provide both management and employees with continuous signals as to what is most important in the day-to-day work and where efforts must be directed. Furthermore, strategically driven departmental measures provide both management and employees with the means to identify with the success of the strategy, and track their own particular contributions to its achievement.

Measures serve both as an informational and motivational tool. Unlike management attention and behavior, which can so readily be distracted and inconsistent, an 'appropriate' set of integrated measures at departmental level provides a steadfast, continuous, and highly visible signal to everyone engaged in making the strategy happen.

Unfortunately, as Drucker and Peters point out, few organizations have come anywhere close to establishing a strategically driven performance measurement system that extends down to department level. Instead, most organizations have in place a hodge-podge collection of measures which have evolved over time. These may or may not be relevant to the current strategies being pursued. Some may even successfully undermine strategy implementation because they focus attention at working levels on the 'wrong' issues (e.g. forcing an undue emphasis on cost reduction when the crucial strategic requirement is faster cycle times to improve time-to-market for new product introductions).

Building a strategic control system

Top management need performance indicators to let them know whether their strategies are on track. Most traditional measures do not help out. As discussed in chapter 2, a fundamentally different approach to measurement and control is imperative.

World-class performance measurement must be designed to keep the focus constantly on strategic business objectives. For continuous and timely feedback at the local department level, the criteria for the measures and the measures themselves must be cast in real-time operational terms instead of strategic or top-level financial terms. Exhibit 3.1 compares some of the fundamental differences between a traditional performance measurement system and a strategic performance measurement system.

Exhibit 3.1 Traditional versus strategic performance measurement systems

Traditional	**Strategic**
Financial focus	*Strategic focus*
• Financially driven (past focus)	• Customer-driven (future focus)
• Limited flexibility; one system serves both external and internal needs	• Flexible, dedicated system for operational control
• Not linked to operations strategy	• Tracks concurrent strategies
• Used to adjust financials	• Catalyst for process improvements
Locally optimized	*Systematically optimized*
• Decrease costs	• Improve performance
• Vertical reporting	• Horizontal reporting
Fragmented	*Integrated*
• Cost, output, and quality viewed in isolation	• Quality, delivery, time, and cost evaluated simultaneously
• Trade-offs unknown	• Trade-offs addressed
Individual incentives	*Group incentives*
• Individual learning	• Organizational learning

Summary

The 1990s will continue to be paced by more global competition, changing technologies, even more emphasis on quality and service, and shorter product lifecycles. These factors will place ever-increasing demands on a company's responsiveness to customer needs. Developing a strategic plan to meet these challenges will be more than a management exercise. It will be necessary for survival.

However, most senior executives have been frustrated by the inability of their organizations to sustain the focus and momentum required over several years to implement the strategies they formulate.

In this chapter, we have argued that performance measurement is the single most powerful mechanism at management's disposal to enhance the probability of successful implementation. Typically, when an organization formulates a strategic plan, it does so at the level of the entire business, treating each function as part of an integrated whole. Yet the actual execution of the strategy occurs primarily at the departmental or functional level. It is crucial, therefore, that managers:

- have a good compass when they load the ship and set off in a new strategic direction
- spend as much time on operational acceptance of strategy – including the institutionalization of the new measures – as they typically do in pilot installations
- continually match day-to-day operational performance measures to the critical success factors articulated in the strategy.

Notes

We are indebted to Arnold Judson, chairman of Gray–Judson–Howard, for his contributions to this chapter.

1 Additional readings: Arnold Judson, *Making Strategy Happen: Transforming Plans Into Reality* (Basil Blackwell, Oxford, 1990); Michael Porter, *Competitive Strategy* (Free Press, New York, 1980); Benjamin Tregoe and John Zimmerman, *Top Management Strategy* (Simon & Schuster, New York, 1980).

4

◇

The Eyes of the Customer

◆

O wad some pow'r the giftie gie us
To see oursels as others see us!

Robert Burns, Scottish Poet

In the last chapter, we stressed the importance of developing your corporate strategy and designing a dynamic yardstick to help keep your strategy on track. Strategy does more than guide the nature and direction of your organization. It also tells you who your customers are.

But managers and employees need more than a general direction and a compass to ensure top performance. Like travellers heading on a new journey, they need a *map* of the business — a clear picture of how work gets done. Maps are also useful tools in plotting the shortest and most economical way to reach your destination. Two Harvard professors echo the importance of mapping in business:

Who would dream of setting off [on a journey into the wilderness] without a map? Of course, you would try to clarify the purpose of the journey and make sure that the needed equipment is available and in order. But once committed to the trip, you need a map of the terrain, something everybody can study — the focus for discussion, the basis for planning alternative courses. Knowing where you've come from and where you are is essential to knowing how to get where you want to go.[1]

With a good map in hand, employees can find a simpler, more direct path to the customer.

- Maps help in understanding the perspective of the customer — the reason your company exists — whether that customer is the end-user or a distribution channel.

39

- Maps also help focus on the internal flow of work to internal customers – the reason your department or function exists – from product/service creation to value being provided to the end-customer.
- In providing a more holistic picture of the way work gets done, maps can also be used to streamline operations.
- Once you understand how you are organized to reach your destination, maps can be used in determining which yardsticks effectively measure the flow of work to improve the value of your company's products or services in the 'eyes of the customer.'

This chapter focuses on the first three uses of a business map. Chapters 5–8 address the problem of how to tailor specific measurements to your workflow.

Service maps: the road to customer satisfaction

In the late 1970s much was written about the shift from manufacturing to service sector jobs – what that meant in terms of the economic base, income, job skills, and the like. Today service is a hot business topic again but with a new twist. Manufacturing companies are quickly learning that to remain competitive, they must become more like service companies.

For example, direct-sell computer companies are no longer judged solely on the quality of the 'hardware' they produce. As CPUs, workstations, and printers become commodities, vendors compete on how well they listen to their customers and the total value and service provided. Customers, end-users in this case, are concerned about several dimensions of the vendor's performance: effectiveness of solution, willingness to customize to a specific need, ease of use, quality of documentation, long-term reliability, responsiveness, effectiveness of maintenance service, technical support provided, availability of software, ease of expansion, and so on.

Some computer manufacturers also sell directly to distribution channels. For example, Apple, Compaq, and IBM sell to retail channels such as ComputerLand. Other computer vendors sell to value-added resellers (VARs). When the 'customer' shifts upstream from the end-user to the distribution channel, the eyes of the customer change focus but the emphasis is still on service. In addition to the products themselves, dealers and VARs are concerned about their satisfaction with profit margins, support charges, marketing support services, quality of information provided, willingness and ability to address dealer/VAR problems, and avoiding cross-channel conflicts.

Whether your customer is a distribution channel or the end-user, both constituencies have to be satisfied. As noted above, these two constituencies are satisfied in two entirely different ways but there is a common theme: *service*.

Some of America's best-run companies – Hewlett-Packard, Allen-Bradley, Caterpillar, and Frito-Lay – are beginning to run their production groups like service factories. Activities are managed from the perspective of how well they serve customers' needs before and after the product is shipped and not just how well the products are made.[2] As this shift takes hold, managers must get to grips with two of the major ramifications related to service focus.

1 Services have a limited ability to buffer customer demand with inventory, therefore they must be very responsive.
2 In a service operation, the customer is more closely involved in the actual service creation process.[3]

When products are viewed as services, your business does not end when the product is sold. As a service business, the service begins with an order and ends only when the customer is satisfied. With this perspective, it becomes possible to identify all the critical points of customer contact with your business.

If all products are seen as a service then what is the distinction between a product-oriented and a service-oriented business? The extent to which employees and customers come in contact is one distinguishing feature. Another feature might be the extent to which the product or service is produced and consumed at the same time. For instance, if one goes to a tax preparation service for tax advice, production and consumption of the product occurs simultaneously with contact between the service provider and the customer. At the opposite end of the spectrum, a candy manufacturer has little or no contact with the customer (end-user) and the product is consumed well after it is produced. Figure 4.1 shows where a number of businesses would fit on a spectrum ranging from high-contact to low-contact businesses and simultaneous versus sequential production and consumption.

Regardless of where your product or service falls in the spectrum depicted in figure 4.1, it is the customer's perspective of your performance that counts. Each time the customer comes in contact with your product, service, or your company it is an opportunity to make a favorable impression (or to create dissatisfaction). At one end of the spectrum, it is the employees that will make or break the opportunity. At the other end of the spectrum, it is the product that will make or break it. The key is to understand when and where those opportunities occur.

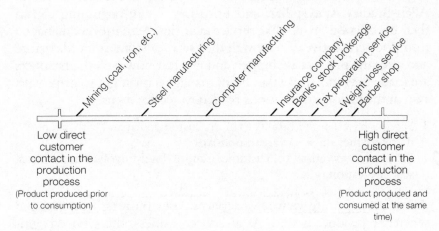

Figure 4.1   The service spectrum

Moments of truth

To describe these points of customer contact and the opportunities presented by them, Jan Carlzon coined the phrase 'moments of truth' (in his book of the same name). A moment of truth is any point at which a customer comes in contact with a business, and the experience can be favorable or unfavorable. For instance, in the case of the tax preparation service there are many moments of truth which are directly controlled by the service provider. In the case of a computer manufacturer, moments of truth tend to occur in the day-to-day use of the machine. However, should something go wrong with the equipment, a major moment of truth can arise when the customer makes a complaint.

At this point, it may be useful to make a distinction between primary and secondary points of contact. The primary points of contact are those moments of truth directly related to the consumption of the product or service. The secondary points of contact are those moments of truth not directly related to the consumption of the product or service. For instance, calling a company with a question or complaint, or receiving a recall letter, are secondary to the actual delivery of the product or service.

For the purpose of performance measurement, it is important to note the points at which there is contact with the customer. These moments of truth will determine customer satisfaction (or dissatisfaction). Only then is it possible to identify the specific attributes of your company's performance which will make or break the opportunities provided by the moments of truth. Understanding the attributes of performance which are important to the customer can go a long way towards instituting an effective performance measurement system. However, recent research has shown that there is a large gap between what an organization thinks it is doing in terms of customer satisfaction and what the customer actually perceives it as doing.[4] Consider the following moment of truth revealed by Scandinavian Airlines System (SAS) president, Jan Carlzon:

The SAS cargo division had always measured its performance by the amount of freight carried . . . this had more to do with an executive suite goal that had nothing to do with the needs of our cargo customers. They were more concerned about precision, or prompt delivery to the specified locations. So we revised our strategy to become the airline with the highest precision. We thought we were doing very well; our cargo people reported that only a small percentage of shipments arrived late. But we decided to try a test anyway . . . and found that shipments were actually four days late on average. Our precision was terrible. We had caught ourselves in one of the most basic mistakes a service oriented business can make: promising one thing and measuring another. In this case, we were promising prompt and precise cargo delivery, yet we were measuring volume and whether or not paperwork and packages got separated en route. In fact, a shipment could arrive four days late without being recorded as a delay.[5]

Mapping can help in the identification of all the major points of contact, or moments of truth, and can lead to effective research regarding customer satisfaction. For each point of customer contact, the following simple questions can be used to help identify the attributes of performance which will satisfy (or dissatisfy) the customer:

- What constitutes good performance?
- What constitutes bad performance?

By viewing your business from the customer's perspective, and seeing what matters to him or her, it is easier to understand what you need to do (or not do) to support your customer.

Customer satisfaction lies behind a double-locked door. Identifying critical customer contacts is the first key; the second key is management of the business activities required to support your customers. These activities can be classified into a few distinct operating systems present in most companies but formally recognized in only a few.

Bureaucracy busters: cross-functional teams

Not all business maps show an easy route to the customer. Many are more like road maps of Boston − narrow streets, one ways, dead ends, and confusing 'rotaries.' Like the bewildered driver reading a Boston map for the first time, employees in bureaucratic snarl-ups also become frustrated.

All too often, organizations get bogged down by their own excess baggage: layers of management, poor teamwork, checkers checking the checkers, and large central staffs who are at some distance from the customer. In a bureaucracy it is likely that yardsticks are used to preserve the status quo, rather than to motivate continuous improvement.

Lawrence Miller pinpoints the problem:

The layered classes of the structure fail to understand each other and are increasingly devoted to their own self interests. The leaders divorce themselves from their followers. The work force proceeds to develop its own bureaucracy to protect itself from unresponsive leadership. The fabric begins to rip.[6]

When bureaucracy becomes a way of life, three things happen within organizations:

1 Employees become isolated from the marketplace customer.
2 The flow of work to the marketplace customer becomes piecemeal, sloppy, and costly − yet no one is held accountable.
3 Creativity and innovation are stifled.

The consequences can be staggering:

In 1989, Wang Laboratories reported a loss of $424 million dollars. When Rick Miller was hired as president of the troubled

*computer maker, in the fall of 1989, he immediately set about
dismantling Wang's internal bureaucracy – a bureaucracy
in which only a handful of the company's new products had any
customer input and workflows were so chaotic and burdened with
unnecessary procedures and reviews that one consultant remarked
that cleaning hazardous waste was less stressful. The environment
discouraged change, turning off employees who tried to do something good for the business.*

Like Wang, many companies lose sight of their customers and the
competition as they grow and mature. As a result, they become de-
tached from the primary business purpose. The best way to spark a
sense of urgency in the organization is to build in to all employees
the principle of customer focus.[7] The starting point for managers to
cut through their internal bureaucracy is that of recognizing the key
business systems that deliver value to the customer.

Business operating systems

To introduce the concept of mapping, we centered on one business
operating system (BOS). In essence, it is the major BOS which receives an order for the product or service and delivers to that order.
For a build-to-order manufacturer, this BOS would include sales
order processing, procurement, production, distribution/shipping,
and installation service (if required). Other examples of BOSs are: a
company's new product introduction cycle (product or service
definition through development and introduction); the after sales
service businesses of many companies; or a company's entire revenue
management cycle, where the service is to the stockholder rather
than the customer.

Note that the emphasis in a BOS is on the horizontal flow of work,
not on the functional specialties. Customers are interested only in
placing an order and getting delivery of that order. They do not care
whether their order is processed through five, seven or ten isolated
functions. Their sole consideration is how effectively the BOS performs as a whole.

It is this day-to-day flow of work throughout an organization until
it reaches the customer that should be managed and measured. New
operational performance indicators should be tailored to the

sequence of activities in the BOS. Attention should be focused on the causal relationships. Unlike MBO and other management techniques, which center on the vertical chains of commands, an effective operational control system must focus on the horizontal workflow regardless of organizational boundaries. In the new operational control environment, the performance focus shifts from interdepartmental competition to teamwork throughout the business system.

A business operating system (BOS) can be defined as all the functions and sequences of activities (wherever they may reside in the organization) required to implement a particular business strategy and deliver a product or service to the customer.

In essence, there are three components to the definition of a BOS.

Sequence of activities

Rather than viewing work as discrete, individual activities, from department to department, think of it as a river flowing continuously, regardless of arbitrary political boundaries, fed by many tributaries. For example, many departments help fill an order: sales, distribution, production, purchasing, and so on. The sales department, however, is involved in the sales order and also the delivery of the product (same source but different tributaries in the river analogy). It is the correct sequence of activities and supporting activities which is crucial to the BOS. In essence, the BOS is a network of internal suppliers and customers throughout the organization that gets the work done.

Implementing a strategy

A business strategy cannot usually be implemented by one department in isolation. A significant business strategy requires the commitment of the entire organization – one stream of activities in day-to-day operations which will have to be managed in order to implement the strategy successfully. For instance, if a new strategy calls for market penetration on the basis of superior service, then marketing, sales, production, and distribution must all work together to achieve that strategy. Likewise, a strategy to reduce time-to-market for a new product must take into account the entire flow of activity, from the point at which the customer's need is identified up to the moment when the first product is produced to meet that need. This strategy would be implemented by an operating system that encompassed the entire new product development cycle.

Delivering a product or service to the customer

A BOS does not just encompass the actual delivery of a product or service. It includes the sequence of activities leading up to the actual delivery of the product or service. For instance, the operating system which delivers the day-to-day product or service may include the advertising process which drives the customer in through the door in the first place.

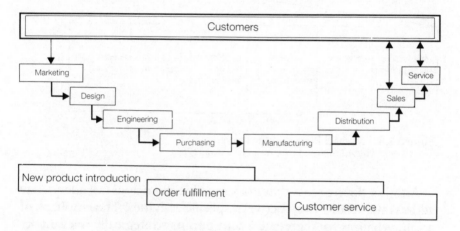

Figure 4.2 Major business operating systems within a business unit (adapted from John F. Rockhart and James E. Short, 'IT in the 1990s: Managing Organizational Interdependence,' *Sloan Management Review*, Winter 1989)

Figure 4.2 depicts the major BOSs in a business unit. There are some similarities and some differences between the BOS concept and Michael Porter's 'value chain' concept. The main difference is that Porter's value chain emphasizes the day-to-day operation of delivering the product or service. For instance, in figure 4.3, a depiction of Michael Porter's value chain, the new product introduction cycle is not called out explicitly. In this example, only one operating system is emphasized: the operating system that processes materials or raw materials as inbound logistics to the point at which the finished product is serviced at the customer's location.

Firm infrastructure					
Human resource management					
Technology development					
Procurement					
Inbound logistics	Operations	Outbound logistics	Marketing and sales	Service	

Margin

Margin

Marketing management	Advertising	Sales force administration	Sales force operations	Technical literature	Promotion

Figure 4.3   Michael Porter's value chain
(from *Competitive Advantage*, Free Press, New York, 1985)

Another difference is that Porter's value chain does not adequately address the relationship between specific activities. The emphasis of a value chain is to 'segregate a firm into its strategically relevant activities in order to understand the behavior of cost and the existing potential sources of differentiation.'[8]

The emphasis of the BOS concept is on the internal and external supplier–customer relationships in order to more effectively deliver value to the customer and to pinpoint the areas where performance indicators are important to the success of the business as a whole.

The value of the BOS concept has been recognized by management in a major chain of fitness centers, XYZ Fitness Corporation. Within the XYZ Fitness business, there are three major operating systems. The first two operating systems are common to most businesses: the new product introduction operating system and the operating system which delivers the service on a day-to-day basis. The third operating system is in essence a revenue management system.

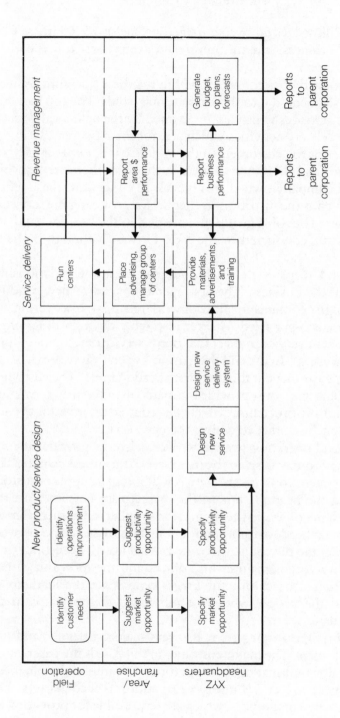

Figure 4.4 XYZ Fitness Corporation: three business operating systems

Figure 4.4 illustrates an oversimplified profile of XYZ Fitness Corporation's business and the interrelationships between the three operating systems.

The major activities contained within the three operating systems have been segmented into three horizontal bands. The top band depicts those activities which are performed by the field locations and are service delivery activities which are, for the most part, visible to the end-user or the customer. In the middle band, between the corporate office and the fitness centers in the field, there are franchise offices and company-owned area offices. In either case, these offices can be viewed as the distribution channel for providing the service to the end-user. The third group of activities, in the bottom band, are those activities conducted by the XYZ Fitness Corporation's headquarters.

Figure 4.4 displays the major supplier–customer relationships throughout the business. The first operating system, 'new product/service design,' contains the flow of work related to discovering and defining a customer need (market research), through designing a new product or service to meet that need (service development, product engineering). In the end this business operating system has a set of primary customers in the corporate headquarters. The customers are the people who must provide the materials, advertising, training, systems, and any procedures which are required in order for the area office or franchise office to deliver the new service.

The second operating system, 'service delivery,' provides the service on a day-to-day basis to the members of the fitness centers. This operating system contains the network of internal supplier–customers, linking the headquarters to the marketplace customer. In this case the first major link in the chain is the supplier–customer relationships between headquarters and the franchise owners, and between headquarters and the company-owned area offices. The second major link is between the area/franchise offices and the individual fitness centers. The customers for the fitness centers are the marketplace consumers, the people who have purchased memberships in the fitness centers.

The third operating system has one major customer and two minor customers. The major customer in this case is the parent company, a major multinational corporation. The minor customers are the managers in XYZ Fitness Corporation's headquarters, area offices, and franchise offices, which are responsible for providing the

service. The parent corporation must be considered the primary customer because the budgets, operating plans, forecasts, and financial
performance reports are done to the parent corporation's specifications. It is the parent corporation which dictates the frequency of,
format of and procedures related to these activities. Therefore, due to
the driving influence of the parent corporation, the revenue management activities have become a distinct operating system.

Prior to the acquisition of XYZ Fitness Corporation by the parent
corporation, financial record-keeping and reporting was just another
routine part of delivering the service. In essence, reporting on center
enrollments, member retention, and financial reporting could be
considered a part of the service delivery system. However, like many
companies which are bought out by a strong parent corporation, the
revenue management system has taken on a mission of its own. The
mission is to support the requirements of the parent company, the
major stockholder of the business. This situation is not unusual.
Other companies not owned by a strong parent corporation may
have similar requirements put on them by stockholder groups, venture capitalists, creditors, bankruptcy courts, or private investment
groups. The important point is to distinguish between an operating
system which supports the customers and an operating system which
may be in place to support the stockholders.

By viewing their business as three distinct operating systems, XYZ
Fitness Corporation recognized the need to emphasize operating
performance in order to achieve financial performance. For instance,
in the service delivery operating system the operating objective is to:
(1) meet the customer's expectations (as defined by the customer);
(2) be flexible enough to match capacity with demand (through op-
timizing availability and staffing of centers); and (3) do both pro-
fitably. However, XYZ Fitness Corporation recognized that its sole
reliance on aggregate financial reports was ineffective in improving
performance. More specific operational measures were needed in
order to more effectively manage the linkages between specific
activities to meet these operating objectives.

For instance, the area office is charged with providing the fitness
centers with materials such as registration cards, customer handouts,
and products which may be sold to the customers. In this scenario,
the area logistics function needed measures related to 'on-time delivery to the right location of the right quantity of undamaged
materials.' Internally, the logistics operation needed measures to

encourage keeping waste to a minimum in terms of inventory, expediting, and rework, and also to encourage internal responsiveness (reduced cycle times).

By taking this BOS perspective on their business, it became apparent to XYZ Fitness Corporation that some 'support' functions, such as the purchasing department, support the primary workflow, but that others, such as information services and human resources, are in fact 'service' functions. Neither is directly involved in the flow of work to and from the customers but their services can help line people be more competitive. For example, human resources helps management hire, reward, punish, or fire the people involved in conducting the activities of the business.

In essence, their customers are the managers and employees who conduct both the primary and support activities contained in the BOS. Likewise, the information service department provides a service by automating the flow of information (which is a big part of the flow of work) and maintaining the automated systems. As such, the information services group provides a service to management in the form of projects and day-to-day service.

When a BOS is not a BOS

There may be a number of reasons why a BOS does not measure up to our definition. One reason might be that the physical location of facilities and the existing flow of work are separate from each other. For example, a major food company headquartered in the Midwest might manufacture much of their canned food in one location but distribute it from another location 1,000 miles away. In this case the company might decide that they in fact have two operating systems, a distribution operating system and a manufacturing operating sys-

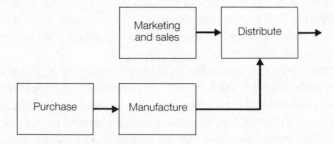

Figure 4.5   Production and distribution business operating systems

tem, even though neither can deliver the product to the customer without the other. Figure 4.5 depicts the flow of work on two levels, where the lower level is a feeder process to the upper level, or distribution system.

The same situation occurs when a manufacturer produces sub-assemblies in one or more locations and delivers the sub-assemblies to a final assembly plant. In this situation many companies have decided that order receipt through final assembly through customer receipt is one operating system. The other operating system or systems are found in the individual sub-assembly plants.

There are circumstances where having two such 'subsystems' makes sense. It may make sense to manufacture the product close to the raw materials and distribute the product close to the marketplace customer. It may also make sense to manufacture sub-assemblies close to the raw materials and produce final assemblies to order close to the customer. However, there is a pitfall. The segmentation into two operating systems will be taken for granted. It will be much more unlikely that serious effort will be put into radically rethinking the flow of work in order to combine the two operating systems into one, as depicted in figure 4.6, which is the essence of JIT manufacturing.

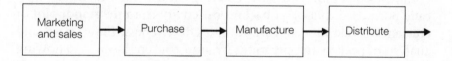

Figure 4.6   JIT production and distribution business operating system

Mapping the way work gets done

A business map is essentially a type of flow chart which depicts the types of activity required to operate a portion of the business or all of the business. In essence, a business map provides clear documentation on the supplier–customer relationship throughout the business. A business map depicts how work gets done.

While system flow charts, operational flow charts, business blueprinting, and business mapping have been around for some time, there is one particular approach which is especially helpful for getting at the appropriate measures of operating performance. In response to its work with service businesses, Gray–Judson–Howard, a consulting firm in Cambridge, Massachusetts, has developed an approach to business mapping which

- highlights all contacts and activities with the end-user
- highlights all contacts and activities with the distribution channel
- highlights the relationship between the backroom activities required to support the distribution channel and end-user

This clear representation of activities ensures that both the end-user and distribution channel contacts are visible and are considered in the development of performance measurements.

This mapping technique represents a combination of service blueprinting and industrial engineering flow charting. Service blueprinting was developed by Lynn Shostack as a mechanism to depict a direct customer contact with a business along with the immediate supporting activities. It was intended as a mechanism to highlight where things would go well (quality and delivery performance) and where things could fail from the customer's perspective. In essence, the company was concerned with how effectively the business system was satisfying the customer.

Industrial engineering flow charting on the other hand has typically been used to look at backroom activity from the standpoint of efficiency (cycle time and waste) not effectiveness. Flow charts and analysis of backroom operations by industrial engineers – showing operations, inspections, movement, delays, and storage – were typically intended to highlight opportunities to reduce costs.

Managed improperly, it is not unusual for cost reductions to hurt revenues (by hurting customer satisfaction) and for revenue enhancement programs to hurt costs. Through the business map the revenue and cost drivers are presented together so that they can be evaluated simultaneously, enabling the process to be redesigned, measured, and managed for profit.

In addition to providing a systematic framework for developing an economic model of the service, the business map acts as a catalyst to profit by facilitating the following.

Communication

The map provides a visual description of the day-to-day process of managing and delivering the total service. As such, it is a significant improvement over prior conceptual verbal definitions. The map reduces the risk of varied and inaccurate descriptions of how the business operates by developing a uniform definition and facilitating a common understanding of the business. The foundation is laid for effective company-wide collaboration on business improvements.

Market research and service design

The map provides an accurate step-by-step portrayal of how the customer (distribution channel and/or end-user) sees the business. These points of contact are highlighted on the map, enhancing management's ability to do well-targeted and focused research on customer satisfaction. The map enables the point of customer contact to be evaluated and redesigned in context of the entire business. Assessing the impact of adding or deleting points of contact or altering the content of a contact point is helped by the map's definition of both the customer's perspective and the operations perspective on one page.

Operations design

The map also enables internal operations or backroom activity to be viewed in the context of the whole business. These activities, which directly or indirectly contribute to the customer's perception of the business, are considered with regard to their contributions to revenues as well as cost.

Information system design

Mapping enables information systems to be designed in the context of the whole business. Maps not only depict customer contacts with the business, the flow of material through the business, or specific activities, but also include the flow of information required to perform many of the activities. New information systems or enhancements to existing information systems can be designed with an eye towards win–win situations, where both costs are reduced and customer satisfaction is enhanced.

Process management

Ideally management should rely more on the process than on the personalities of its people. After all, as Dr Juran has pointed out, 80 percent of the problems in companies are related to process and system problems that are manager-controllable.[9] The mapping approach can provide a clear definition of how a process should work. Clarity of process enables the development of effective policies, procedures, and/or guidelines. Operations manuals and training programs can be structured to articulate clearly the activity desired at each step of the process.

Performance measurement

The business map pinpoints opportunities to institute clear measures and controls. A perspective on the business as a whole enables measures to be designed to meet the best strategic balance between service quality, product quality, and profitability and not just measure the false efficiencies of individual functions. Performance measures are most effective when controlling the horizontal flow of work as depicted by the map and when unconstrained by the vertical flow of organizational power. The map provides this perspective by focusing on all of these activities in a continuous flow rather than on organizational boundaries.

Features of a typical business map

The illustration of XYZ Fitness Corporation's business operating systems presented in figure 4.4 is an oversimplified business map, using generic legends. Other flow charting techniques, such as systems flow charting and industrial engineering flow charting, use different symbols but achieve a similar objective. The figure does have some of the typical features of a business map. The business map is divided into horizontal bands, which are used to organize activities into categories of strategic and operational significance. These bands enable the map to be scanned more easily and important points highlighted.

A typical business map contains:

- an end-user band, which charts the sequential service processes through which an end-user flows; if the end-user of the service is

considered the customer, the band could be labelled 'customer contact'
- a distribution channel band, which charts the sequential service processes through which an intermediary delivers the service from the company to an end-user; if the distribution channel is the customer, the band could be labelled 'customer contact'
- a backroom activity band, which charts the non-visible service activities that support and facilitate the sequential processes in the customer contact band; this band offers the first opportunity of visualizing elements of the operating strategy and their link to the customer
- (sometimes) a management report band, which highlights how collected data is fed back to managers − usually in the form of reports.

The business map is much like a road map in that it displays a variety of possible paths. The major highways are emphasized, yet the offshoots and back roads which are less traveled are also displayed.

The intention of the business map is to display the normal progression of work as if looking down on the business from a high vantage-point. In many cases, there is a symbol (superimposed on the path) to signify the type of work which is flowing. For instance, a telephone symbol is placed over the line between the point at which a customer may telephone the business and that at which there is backroom activity involving the information generated by that telephone call.

Like a road map, the business map shows the paths and their inter-relationships but not the capacities or usage of those paths. Understanding the capacities of both the paths and the activities, and also understanding the load of work on those paths and activities, is critical to any attempt at improving or redesigning a process.

For performance measurement, the map needs to be sufficiently detailed so as to represent the major inputs to the operating system as well as the major outputs. Also like a road map, the detail can vary depending on the information needs of the user: a road map may show only the major interstate highways or it may detail all the streets on a particular block. It is important to depict all the major activities required to transform and process the flow of work from beginning to end of each operating system. The level of detail should be sufficient to highlight the major steps involved in transforming the work or in transforming and integrating information. Typically these

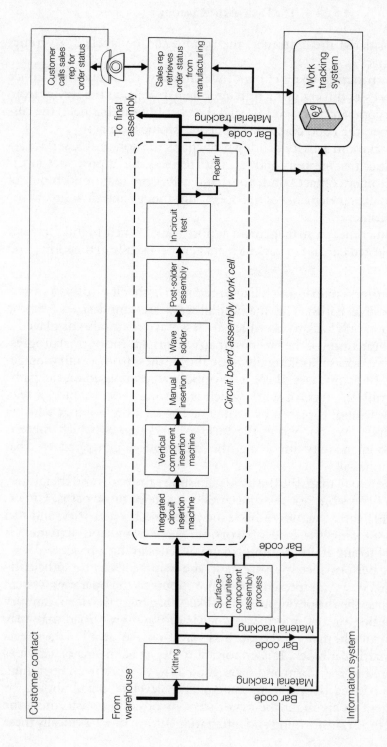

Figure 4.7 Workflow through a manufacturing department

major steps or activities can be identified as work centers. In effect, the task is to identify all the significant internal supplier–customer relationships that occur within the operating system and within the departments contained in the BOS. Note that the emphasis is on activities required to perform the work not on the departmental boundaries.

It is critical to identify any contact between the external customer of the business and the department, even if that contact is indirect. For example, although a manufacturing department may perceive itself as invisible to the end-customer, the customer may telephone the sales organization to inquire about an order's delivery date. Sales may then telephone manufacturing to check on the status of the order. If manufacturing cannot respond in a timely and accurate fashion, then customer satisfaction objectives for both sales and the company will not be achieved. Identifying these points of contact on the flow chart will help to ensure that adequate consideration is given to establishing measures which are relevant to those contacts. A simplified example of a manufacturing department's workflow is illustrated in figure 4.7. Note that this illustration also contains an information systems band, which is sometimes critical in depicting a map of a manufacturing business.

In some respects, the process of developing the flow chart may be more important than the flow chart itself. Developing the flow chart is an effective vehicle for clearly identifying not only the points of customer contact and transfer of work but also the people who should be involved in discussing the performance measures for those points.

The most important feature of the map is the clear articulation of the internal supplier–customer relations throughout the BOS. With all the key internal supplier–customer relations identified, it then becomes possible to institute an effective measurement and control system. Critical success measures must be identified where the two functions touch. Using this approach, it is possible to focus attention not only on how effectively each group operates but, more importantly, on how each group works *together* in meeting the customer's needs and expectations.

Streamlining your business systems

Once the map is developed what do you do with it? You could frame it, hang it on the wall, and point to it as an illustration of how the business operates today. Or you could analyze it, develop and test various hypotheses about how the workflow could be streamlined, eventually drawing conclusions and making recommendations about how operations could be improved. In many cases, the map could be used as a catalyst to alter the structure of the business. Where possible, these opportunities to restructure the business should be done prior to instituting performance measures. The following case study illustrates the point.

A Fortune 500 manufacturer had recognized for some time that product margins and market share were eroding. When the vice-presidents of R&D and manufacturing got together to do a 'post-mortem' on why a strategic product was six months late, they were not happy campers. They called for process changes that would reduce throughput time for new product introductions, without limiting their capability of introducing strategic new products. Specific goals were defined: time-to-market was to be cut in half, waste was to be eliminated, people were to be held accountable and cross-functional teams were to report to one leader. The first step of the project was to map the existing workflow. When an industrial engineer presented his findings to senior management, the manufacturing vice-president quipped that it was amazing any new products could be introduced at all. The R&D vice-president began asking questions about the symbols on the map. The walls were covered with industrial engineering symbols of delays, moves, inspections, and storage. It was painfully obvious that very little time in the product development cycle was adding any value. The development chief, appalled by the morass, called for changes in the workflow. In less than three months, a small product and process design team redesigned the workflow for the introduction of new products. They had cut development time in half and eliminated redundant activities and jobs. After the initial success, when cycle times started to creep back up, the team then put in performance measures for on-time delivery, cycle time, and quality, and reviewed them on a weekly basis. Everybody focused their attention on the same map, all looking for faster ways to get to the market.

A map of your business may provide similar surprises, by unearthing a number of problems, issues, and opportunities. In addition to helping you focus on the customer and understand the customer's expectations, mapping also helps you to streamline operations.

More specifically, this mapping technique has been especially effective at helping numerous businesses to:

- uncover activities and information flows that should be modified or eliminated
- assess the backroom impact (cost, timing, steps, confusion, etc.) of introducing different kinds of new services and products
- design operating specifications and/or guidelines for each step in the service or product delivery system
- highlight problem areas where corrective action can be taken
- assess true activity-based product costs
- assist the information systems department in systems design
- highlight opportunities to link flows of information and activities.

For readers interested in more information on workflow simplification principles, we have provided supplementary material in Appendix A.

Summary

At the beginning of this chapter we stated two primary reasons for mapping the activities in your organization:

1 To help your organization be more effective in the eyes of the customer.
2 To help you simplify the way work gets done.

In a general sense, your customers see your business as two or three major operating systems, such as new product introduction, delivery of product or service, and/or providing after sales support in service. In a specific sense there are points of contact, or moments of truth, where the customer encounters your business, and each point of contact is a make or break opportunity. Mapping identifies both, and forms a blueprint for measures of customer satisfaction. It shows the responsiveness of the BOS as a whole and that of the individual departments and workcells within it.

The second reason for mapping is to understand the flow of work to the customer and to make it more efficient. When customers order a product or service they do not care whether it passes through five or six functions and/or five or six layers of management before they take delivery of it. The movement of work from beginning to end is what counts, regardless of the functions, layers, levels, and departments through which the work must flow. Business mapping provides the means to document, analyze, and improve the flow of work. The key is to manage the horizontal flow of work, not the vertical chain of command.

With a map in hand, the task of changing your performance yardsticks will be much easier.

Notes

1 Steven C. Wheelwright and W. Earl Sasser Jr, 'The New Product Development Map,' *Harvard Business Review*, May–June 1989. Although the authors are referring to a 'product map,' the same holds true for business system maps.
2 Richard B. Chase and David A. Garvin, 'The Service Factory,' *Harvard Business Review*, July–August 1989.
3 Jeffrey G. Miller, Alfred J. Nanni, and Thomas E. Vollmann, 'Rethinking Manufacturing Equations With Just-In-Time' (Boston University, 1986).
4 'Customer Focus Research Study' (The Forum Corporation, Boston, Mass., 1988).
5 Jan Carlzon, *Moments of Truth* (Balinger, Cambridge, Mass., 1987).
6 Lawrence M. Miller, *Barbarians to Bureaucrats* (Clarkson N. Potter Inc., New York, 1989).
7 Ibid.
8 Michael Porter, *Competitive Advantage* (Free Press, New York, 1985).
9 J.M. Juran, *Juran on Quality Improvement* (Juran Institute, New York, 1981).

5

◇

Down to Brass Tacks

◆

Information shared becomes knowledge.

Vigorous global competition, product proliferation, shorter product lifecycles, and advanced product and process technologies have forever changed the formula for success in business. Managing in the 1990s will require a new management philosophy and new tools to be successful.

Some companies are already making the transition. For example, in its landmark book, *Made in America*, the MIT Commission on Industrial Productivity noted several 'best practices' in successful companies:

- simultaneous improvement in quality, cost, and speed of new product development
- competitive benchmarking
- close ties with customers and suppliers
- greater functional integration and less organizational stratification (flatter organizations)
- training and continuous learning.

The new yardsticks play a vital role in each of these areas by building on three general basic premises about performance.

- First, operations are linked to strategic goals by translating aggregate market and financial goals into operational terms for each business system (e.g. new product introduction, order fulfillment) and then into concrete operational measures for each department or component of those systems.

63

- Second, items of financial and non-financial information are integrated and filtered so that operating managers can use the information as a catalyst for process improvement. Key measures in terms of quality, delivery, and cycle time are viewed alongside cost performance. However, from an operational perspective cost is viewed in terms of waste in the process.
- Third, all business activities focus on the needs of the customer by communicating changing quality and delivery demands from the downstream customers to the upstream departments in the business system.

The performance pyramid

From an external point of view, the customer and the stockholder determine what it is important to measure. The competition determines how good your performance in those measures needs to be. Successful manufacturers and service companies alike have been competing on three fronts: customer satisfaction, flexibility, and productivity. A valuable lesson from the Japanese is the order that the weapons are mastered: customer satisfaction first, productivity second, and then flexibility! A legitimate concern for many Western companies is that they must play catch-up on all three fronts.

The emphasis on customer satisfaction has been seen in everything from advertising (Chrysler's 'Satisfy the customer' and Ford's 'Quality is job no. 1' are just two examples) to employee-of-the-month programs. Numerous companies are instituting quality programs such as those offered by the PA consulting group, the Juran Institute, and Philip B. Crosby's PCA Inc.

Not long ago, companies had fewer products with longer life-spans. Today, many are competing on new turf: variety and customization. The two terms have similar connotations, but are really quite different. Variety means offering the customer more choice of commodity product. For example, one of the nation's large steel producers offers over 60 varieties of stainless steel. Similarly, in the now famous Honda–Yamaha variety war, Honda introduced/replaced 113 motorcycle models in 18 months, whereas Yamaha managed to introduce only 37, forcing Yamaha to 'surrender.'[1] Other companies may choose to compete on customization by standardizing the commodity but customizing the services that surround it.[2]

Flexibility is certainly a major competitive advantage. JIT techniques are drastically reducing throughput time. For example, Toyota suppliers' turnaround time has been cut from 15 days to same-day delivery. Motorola produces pagers in just two hours, a job that took three weeks just a few years ago. Computer-integrated manufacturing is allowing rapid changeover for increased responsiveness. The Marysville Honda plant can change car models without missing a beat. Flexibility also is seen in the emphasis on time-to-market. Companies such as Hewlett-Packard are introducing new products in half the time.

While customer satisfaction and flexibility are new fronts in the battle for tomorrow's customers, fighting on the third front – productivity – has increased in intensity. Global competition and eroding margins in mature industries have forced companies to restructure and to do more with less.

The performance pyramid shown in figure 5.1 represents the linkage in the new information network. A four-level pyramid of objectives and measures ensures an effective link between strategy and

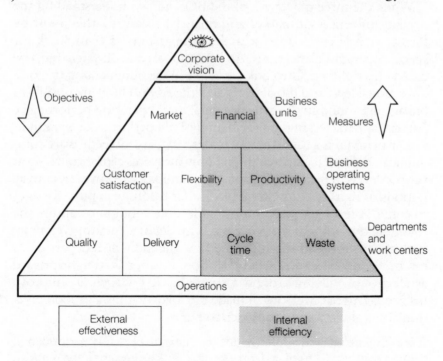

Figure 5.1 The performance pyramid

operations by translating strategic objectives from the top down
(based on customer priorities) and measures from the bottom up. It
represents a new paradigm of performance for many companies.

At the top level, a vision for the business is articulated by corporate
senior management. At the second level, objectives for each business
unit are then defined in market and financial terms. Strategies are
then formulated, describing how these objectives will be achieved. At
the third level, for each BOS supporting the business strategy, more
tangible operating objectives and priorities can be defined in terms of
'customer satisfaction,' 'flexibility,' and 'productivity.' At the base of
the pyramid, objectives are converted into specific operational
criteria: 'quality,' 'delivery,' 'cycle time,' and 'waste' for each department or component of the business system.

The performance pyramid illustrates the principal relationships
between these objectives and the marketing and financial goals of
business units at the second level of the pyramid. Market measures,
in other words, are supported by both 'customer satisfaction' and
'flexibility.'

While the three objectives of the BOS help in understanding the
driving influences of market and financial measures, they must be
further translated to provide a clear foundation or framework for
specific operational measures. An operational control system must be
based on a tightly defined linkage between measurements at the local
operational level and the objectives of the BOS. The elements of this
linkage are found in the four principal local operating performance
criteria, as depicted in the fourth level of the performance pyramid.

The pyramid is a useful model to describe how objectives are communicated down to the troops and how measures can be rolled up at
various levels in the organization. A pyramid does, however, convey
notions of rigidity – limestone blocks put painfully in place for ages
to come. A feedback system must be flexible enough to capture the
changing dynamics of the process it is modelling. At any given time,
both the priorities of the BOS and how the individual departments
can best contribute must be understood. It is not as straightforward
as all groups rallying around a single battle cry such as 'Improve
delivery!' Duncan McDougall made the following insightful observation about the Japanese approach to metrics:

It is as though you can't improve just one measure of factory performance,
because they are all linked, as by slack ropes. Pick an area for improvement,
such as lead time, and start pulling on it. It moves a little, but not far before

something stops it . . . a tug from another area of performance. Perhaps the work-in-process inventory is so great that improving lead time on one product causes others to be later, yielding no net gain. So you turn the organization's attention to reducing WIP. And when someone asks, 'Why are we working on inventory reduction?' you respond, 'Because it is necessary to reduce lead time, which is our sole manufacturing goal.'[3]

Visions of tomorrow

Figure 5.2 A vision sets the context for measuring performance

A vision lays bare the heart and soul of a company as well as setting its strategic course. It defines the markets in which and the basis on which the company will compete. A company's vision and strategy directly translate into how the company plans to reach its goals and what measures are truly critical to the plan's success. Some of the major bases of competition are listed below.

Price, price discrimination

While price is important to the customer, it is not an operational performance measure. Price is a management decision based upon operational performance criteria, combined with dictates of the marketplace. For instance, low cost across all departments and functions will also allow for lower pricing.

Product innovation, product differentiation, product breadth of
line, product quality, product availability

Today many products are becoming commodities and the transfer of
production technology is routine. As a result, companies are seeking
competitive advantage from new product introductions, customized
solutions, and shorter quoted lead times.

Quality of salesforce, point-of-sale services, after sales service,
financial aid to customers, point-of-sale amenities

For many companies the focus of competition has shifted to service
value, given product design, quality, and price. Winning over tomorrow's customers requires a new set of additional services, including
rapid response, logistics support, more rapid design change and providing solutions to customers' needs, not just supplying products.[4]

The importance of having a clear vision has not been ignored by
the business press. In his book *Making Strategy Work*, Richard G.
Hamermesh states: 'Vision is what has directed IBM's total attention
to the opportunities created by the advent of data processing; it is a
specific concept of what a company is trying to become.'[5] His book
also refers to Fred Gluck's description of vision:

the visions of the successful, excellent companies we have discussed were
based not only on a clear notion of the markets in which they would compete, but also on specific concepts of how they would establish an econom-
ically attractive and sustainable role or position in that market. They were
powerful visions grounded in deep understanding of industry and competitive dynamics, and company capabilities and potential. They were not mere
wishful thinking as is the case with so many incomplete visions . . . the
visions were generally directed at continually strengthening the company's
economic or market positions or both in some substantial way.[6]

Three examples of vision statements were presented by Ken Andrews
in his book *The Concept of Corporate Strategy*.[7]

Heublein

Heublein aims to market in the US and via franchise overseas a
wide variety of high-margin, high-quality consumer products
concentrated in the liquor and food business, especially bottled
cocktails, vodka, and other special-use and distinctive beverages

and specialty convenience foods, addressed to a relatively prosperous, young-adult market and returning over 15 percent of equity after taxes. With emphasis on the techniques of consumer goods marketing (brand promotion, wide distribution, product representation in more than one price segment and very substantial off-beat advertising directed closely to its growing audience) Heublein intends to make Smirnoff the number one liquor brand worldwide and to maintain a sales growth of 10 percent a year worldwide via internal growth or acquisitions or both. Its manufacturing policy rather than full integration is in liquor to redistill only to bring purchased spirits up to high quality standards. It aims to finance its internal growth through the use of debt and its considerable cash flow and to use its favorable price earnings ration for acquisitions. Both its liquor and food distribution are intended to secure distributor support through advertising and concern for the distributor's profit.

Mr Keller's Watch Company (*not the real name*)

It is Mr Keller's present plan to produce watches of the highest quality, in a price range between the hand-made ultra-exclusive level and Omega and Rolex. He aims to distribute his watches to all markets of the free world via exclusive wholesale agents and carefully chosen retailers, who are expected to convince customers of the particular value of the product.

His growth of about 10 percent per year is not geared to demand but is deliberately restricted to the productivity of available skilled labor, and to his recognition of cyclical fluctuations in the industry.

Crown Cork and Seal

Crown Cork and Seal aims to be a stripped-down and increasingly profitable manufacturer of specialty high-margin rigid containers for hard-to-hold applications (aerosol products and beer) and to maintain its position in bottling machinery and crowns. Its domestic growth will come from increasing the number of geographically decentralized small plants equipped and located to provide fast delivery at low transportation cost and to secure 20–40 percent of each local market. Customer service is led by a technically trained salesforce alert to customer needs and by a technical 'research' and manufacturing engineering organization, which is solving current customer process and packing problems rather than doing basic research. Its current investment in innovation is kept small, but an aggressive marketing and a flexible manufacturing organization are keen to promote advances pioneered by major suppliers and competitors. Domestic operations are intended to be the stable base from which the company can expand internationally. The developing countries to which crown manufacture has already been introduced are expected to be the company's major growth opportunity in containers. Operations will be financed through retained earnings and full use of debt capacity and are expected to return 25 cents additional profit per share per year. The organization will reward drive, energy, and accomplishment and accept rapid turnover in management ranks whenever results fall below expectations.

The following is a more recent example of the power of visioning:

Seiko Watches

Seiko had a vision that watches are a fashion business, not a time-keeping business. As a fashion company, they needed frequent new products and made strategic investments in computer-integrated manufacturing. Today they introduce three new watches a day and dominate the market they helped to create.

Strategic business unit objectives

In order for the company as a whole to reach its vision, each of the business units and/or divisions must play their part. Separate businesses in large, usually diversified companies, make it easier to make independent decisions regarding market share, cost structure, and workflow. Strategic business units (SBUs) make sense when the following criteria are met: (1) the unit has distinct business concepts and missions; (2) it has its own competitors; (3) its competitors are external; and (4) it is better off managing its strategies in an independent manner.

Most business units define success in terms of: (1) achieving the long-term goals of growth and market position; and (2) achieving the short-term goals of specified levels of positive cash flow and profitability.

Figure 5.3   Business unit goals and measures criteria

Market objectives

Market measures are external measures, driven by the customer. They include:

- absolute market share
- relative market share
- market share rank
- share to largest competitor.

Longer-term market measures would also include measures of innovation:

- new product sales and percentage of market
- R&D spending
- percentage of market with major changes in technology.[8]

Financial objectives

While traditional performance measures have emphasized the right-hand side of the performance pyramid, at best they represent only half the picture. Still, financial measures are valid top-level measures for the business as a whole and for each of its business units:

- profitability
- cash flow
- return on investment.

What must change is the overemphasis of these measures in the short run and how the objectives get translated into day-to-day operations.

East meets West: balancing market and financial objectives at the top

On the competitive battlefield, one key strategic measure emerges when the generals of the East meet those of the West: the importance of market share. Table 5.1 shows the difference.

Table 5.1 Ranking of corporate objectives: US versus Japan

Objective	US	Japan
Return on investment	8.1	4.1
Share-price increase	3.8	0.1
Market share	2.4	4.8
Improve product portfolio	1.7	2.3
Rationalization of production and distribution	1.5	2.4
Increase equity ratio	1.3	2.0
Ratio of new products	0.7	3.5
Improve company's image	0.2	0.7
Improve working conditions	0.1	0.3

Executives of 291 Japanese companies and 227 US companies ranked factors from 10, for most important, to 1, for least important.
Source: J. C. Abegglen and G. Stalk Jr, *Kaisha: The Japanese Corporation* (Basic Books, New York, 1985), p. 177.

Japanese managers give much more emphasis to the market measures – market share and ratio of new products (future market share) – than do their American counterparts, and they treat return on investment on a more equal basis. US executives tend to be singularly focused: the financial measures of return on investment and share-price increase dominate their attention. Market share is placed a distant third, and new products ratio is barely in the running.

Getting it done in the middle

The BOS described in chapter 4 is the bridge between the top-level, traditional indicators and the new day-to-day operational measures in the new paradigm. A BOS includes all internal functions, activities, policies and procedures, and supporting systems (e.g. planning and control, information, rewards, communication, etc.) required to implement a particular business strategy, involving the development, production, and provision of specific products or services to particular markets – wherever these may reside in the total organization.

Figure 5.4 BOS objectives and measures criteria

For example, there is a BOS for the new product introduction process (i.e. product definition and product development). Likewise there is a BOS for the order fulfillment cycle that processes orders and ships products. Other examples include customer service and revenue management.

The BOS is the starting-point for effective measurement and control at the departmental level. It is the link between each specific department's performance and the overall strategy and performance of the business, enabling departmental measures to focus on the effectiveness of the entire operating system rather than on the efficiency of a single department.

One department may serve more than one operating system. For instance, one company's printed circuit board fabrication shop served an operating system related to the development and prototype of new circuits yet also served a system involved in fulfilling production orders. The objectives for each operating system, and therefore the indicators of successful performance, might be radically different.

In summary, recognition of the BOS provides all employees with:

- a unified purpose
- a shared sense of a larger mission
- a sense of urgency
- the flexibility to focus on what counts the most.

Right as a trivet

As noted in figure 5.1, customer satisfaction, flexibility, and productivity represent the three-legged trivet upon which top company objectives are balanced. Yet it is not unusual for one of these factors to receive more attention than the others.

'Customer satisfaction' as a driving force

At the BOS level, customer satisfaction signifies how customer expectations are managed. For many operating systems, especially those that support the external customer directly, customer satisfaction is of paramount importance. For the business as a whole, customer satisfaction can be defined in the operating terms of quality and delivery performance.

An operating system driven by customer satisfaction places strong emphasis on the market side of the performance pyramid. A customer-driven operation also impacts the measurement of workflow from department to department. In a customer-driven operating system there is more emphasis on the external measures of quality and delivery from department to department. For instance, 'trial manufacturing' may be primarily concerned with process and product quality, which in turn will improve flexibility and productivity in volume production.

'Flexibility' as a driving force

Flexibility is at the heart of the performance pyramid because it addresses the responsiveness of the operating system. It is not an excuse for chaos. Ultimately, an operating system is said to be flexible if it can efficiently meet the changing demands of its customers. Flexibility has both internal and external components. The external component relates to meeting the demands of the customer. The internal component relates to doing that efficiently. Therefore flexibility objectives should follow customer satisfaction and productivity. That is not to say they are less important, but doing the wrong things faster will impair the other dimensions of performance. For example, an operating system which delivers a product to a customer can meet the customer's requirement by having everything in inventory. To the customer, the operating system would appear flexible but in reality it is not. A truly responsive operating system should be able to produce and deliver to order to satisfy demand without adding to total costs.

Flexibility is being touted as the next competitive battle, implying that customer satisfaction and productivity have been won. In fact, there is ample evidence that many Japanese manufacturers have set flexibility as their number one priority. A survey of North America, Europe, and Japan, indicates that Japanese companies are ahead in the introduction and use of flexible manufacturing systems (FMSs), JIT programs to reduce lead times in manufacturing, improved new product introduction, set-up time reduction (e.g. Toyota's Single Minute Exchange of Dies (SMED)), and expanded job definitions for all workers.[9]

'Productivity' as a driving force

Productivity refers to how effectively resources (including time) are managed in order to achieve the customer satisfaction and flexibility objectives.

Productivity is typically the driving force when firms compete on the basis of price in a commodity market. It is an internally driven force, with much focus on the financial side of the performance pyramid. It is not directly perceived by the customer; however, of the three driving forces, it is often productivity that gets most of the attention. Productivity should be viewed in the context of the most cost effective and timely means of achieving the customer satisfaction and flexibility objectives.

Two kinds of BOS measures

There are really two kinds of measures at the operating system level. One kind is global in nature, covering a wide scope of activities. Global measures provide top management with a sense of whether strategic objectives are being achieved. They are monitored month-to-month or quarter-to-quarter. In a sense they keep management in touch with the outside world. The other kinds of measures are more specific to the internal work flow. They represent day-to-day measures of operating effectiveness and efficiency. They are calculated by rolling up the four performance measures in each department. In a sense, this provides an internal tracking mechanism to the outside, global measures.

Global measures

Global measures may be reported externally (e.g. by independent survey, such as the rating of hotels) or internally (e.g. by service evaluation cards to be filled in by guests staying at the hotel). They may be a combination of two or more of the four performance criteria at the base of the performance pyramid. For example, 'inventory turns' (see exhibit 5.1) has both a delivery and cycle time component. Similarly 'total factor productivity' (outputs/inputs) has both delivery and cost components. Global-type measures also tend to spill over boundaries and summarize the performance of the company as a whole. For example, a product rating may relate to design, manufacture, or after sales service. Exhibit 5.1 provides examples of global measures for the BOS.

Specific workflow measures

The performance pyramid is based on concrete, specific measures that managers and workers can control on a day-to-day basis. If each department in a BOS is reporting on quality, delivery, cycle time, and waste, it is easy to use the data to assess the BOS as a whole. Since quality and delivery measures for the BOS are determined by the end-customer, they are reflected in the external measures taken by the last department of the process. In other words, the entire BOS performs only as well as the performance of the department furthest downstream. As a means of measuring success, this approach re-

---

Exhibit 5.1 Global BOS measures

Customer satisfaction
Lapse rate (insurance company)
Renewal rate (publishing company)
Retention rate (health club)
Revenue per customer
Number of complaints
Customer ratings from surveys
(independent and company sponsored)
Customer intent to repurchase

Flexibility
Quoted lead times
On-time delivery for rush orders
Inventory turns
Development speed (time-to-market)
Rapid design changes
Volume and mix attainment to orders
(responsiveness of production process)
Numbers of products using common
processes (flexibility of production
process design)

Productivity
Total factor productivity (outputs/inputs)
Cost of sales
Selling and general administrative
expenses
Product margins
Expense ratios
Asset turnover ratio
Day sales outstanding
Added value per employee
Break-even time

---

quires local management to focus on the needs of the department next in the process and the overall values set by the paying customer.

The process time measurement for the BOS would be the sum of the critical path cycle times in each department. Cost in the BOS could also be shown as the dollarized sum of each department's waste. However, it is important to tie cost (the operational variable) in to the financial reports to avoid mixed signals. Adding a global-type productivity measure such as total factor productivity to the sum of all waste is one solution. For example, a plant could report the ratio of total costs over output at the BOS level (e.g. a plant) but report waste (scrap, rework, work-in-process) at the department level. With this type of reporting and interaction among departments, managers are not penalized for 'exceeding budget' if overall system costs are lowered.

Measuring the right stuff in the trenches

Any effective control system must be based on a tightly defined linkage between measurements at the local operational level and the objectives and priorities of the BOS. The elements of this linkage are found in four principal local operating performance criteria: quality, delivery, cycle time, and waste (see the fourth level of the performance pyramid). The objective of any function or department in the BOS is to increase quality and delivery, and to decrease cycle time and waste.

Figure 5.5   Department and work center performance criteria

Once the base of the performance pyramid is defined in terms of four performance criteria, it is important to understand the behavior of, and interaction between, these criteria. Performance measures are either (1) external measures, important to the operation's customer (quality and delivery), or (2) internal measures, not directly perceived by the customer, but critical to the operation's ultimate success (cycle time and waste).

With external measures, you always want to improve the company's delivery performance and the quality of the product or service provided. The higher the score, therefore, the better. Internal measures are similar to the cost drivers used in activity-based costing (set-up time, inspection time, rework time, etc.). Operations motivated to meet customer requirements efficiently (fast, no waste) also reduce the cost of the product. They can be measured so that the lower the score, the better (as in golf, where fewer swings and less walking off-course mean that you are playing a better game).

Tangible external measures

Quality

Meeting customer expectations (internal and external) 100 percent of the time through the delivery of defect-free products or services. It is no longer acceptable to think of quality as conformance to specifications. Quality has a far broader meaning in today's marketplace. Quality has to do with features, performance, durability, reliability, aesthetics, perceived quality, etc.

Figure 5.6   External performance criteria

Examples: parts per volume accepted by materials; percentage of good components in final assembly; percentage of problem-free installs (first attempt); cycle count accuracy; planning accuracy;

numbers of vendors or parts on ship-to-stock; completeness of manu-facturing transfer package from R&D.

Delivery

The quantity of product or service delivered on time to the customer, user, next department, as defined by the customer. As JIT takes hold in more and more companies, 'on time' means just that. Shipping early is as unacceptable as shipping late. Good delivery results when performance equals expectations. There are two aspects of delivery: quantity and timeliness. The objective is to align performance with expectations. For instance, the customer and supplier may negotiate and agree on a percentage to be delivered to schedule and a percent-age to be delivered on demand. There will inevitably be some give-and-take regarding both the customer's expectations and the supplier's agreement regarding performance. Once a promise date is agreed to, it in effect becomes a contract.

Examples: percentage delivered to schedule; percentage delivered to rush order; percentage first customer ship on time.

Tangible internal measures

Cycle time

The sum of process time, move time, inspect time, queue time, and storage time. Only process time is considered to be 'value-added' time. Throughput time also captures the same meaning.

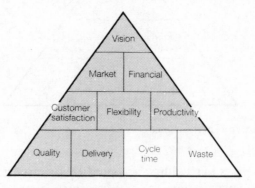

Figure 5.7 Internal performance criteria

Typically only 5 percent of the total cycle is devoted to adding value. In many cases, the product or service is waiting to be worked on 95 percent of the time. The same is true for paper transactions as well! There is a lot of opportunity for improvement and much can be done by focusing on cycle time reduction. Unnecessarily long cycle time contributes directly to poor strategic performance regarding productivity and flexibility.

Examples: time-to-market; development time; manufacturing lead time; department throughput time; workstation set-up time.

Waste

The non-value-added activities and resources incurred in meeting the requirements of the customer. Waste includes all the effort and costs associated with failures, appraisals, and surpluses.

This definition has some major implications. It means that effort expended in repairing defects or in producing 110 units to get out 100 good ones is not poor quality performance, it is poor cost performance. These problems are internal in that it is money and effort spent in getting the product right before it is passed on to the customer (downstream department). At the BOS level, the main objective is to improve productivity by reducing overall costs. At the departmental level, the objective becomes more specific: measure and eliminate waste.

Examples: cost of rejected materials; rework; in-process scrap; incoming inspection; warranty costs; surpluses; accidents; returns.

High-quality products or services (based on customer-driven target values) and regular on-time delivery are the paths to customer satisfaction. The combination of externally driven delivery (when the customer wants to take delivery of a product or service) and internally driven cycle time (how we can reduce the time taken to make the product or provide the service) defines flexibility. Productivity goals can be achieved by reducing both cycle time and cost. At the local department level, cost is viewed as the non-value-added costs (or waste) incurred so as to meet the other performance objectives.

It is important to emphasize the significance of *cycle time*. First, it is entirely within a department's control. Second, it has a powerful influence on flexibility, which is rapidly becoming the competitive factor in the industry. Third, it also has a major effect on productivity. In fact, the 'new math of productivity points to time as a manufacturers' most precious resource.'[10]

The operational measures – quality, delivery, cycle time, and waste – are the four pillars of the pyramid and the key to achieving the higher-level results.

Here is how the pyramid works in a manufacturing setting. A JIT strategy is put in place. At the top level is the financial measure return on assets. At the BOS level it is supported by inventory turns, while at the department level, cycle time and waste (which includes costs of inventory) are reported.

Heat-seeking missiles

Performance measurement systems can no longer focus solely on past performance. Rather than looking in the rear mirror, managers must learn how to read the road ahead. Stan Davis, author of *Future Perfect*, likens control systems of tomorrow to heat-seeking missiles that are capable of in-flight correction to stay on track of the elusive target ahead.

Strategic control takes the tracking and checking up characteristics of the control function, and rather than locating them in what has already happened, it places them in the future. It continually tracks how the future 'X' is changing as you get closer to it, so that, although you are still managing to stated future objectives, the objectives are updated daily to correspond to the shifting reality.[11]

Figure 5.8 forms the basis for such a strategic performance measure system. This model is a powerful mechanism for managers to make sure their day-to-day performance measures are tracking close to their external targets.

A note about critical success factors

The term 'critical success factors,' or CSFs, was popularized in the late 1970s by John F. Rockart of MIT's Sloan Management School.[12] The concept grew out of an information systems research project to help executives define their significant information needs. In a sense, the concept of CSFs was an extension of earlier works in the areas of management control systems and management information systems

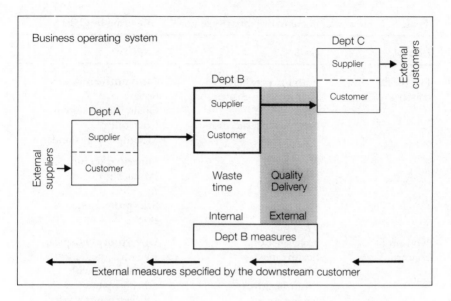

Figure 5.8   Guidance system to keep measures on track

(MISs).[13] At the time, CSFs were seen as a breakthrough approach to help executives focus on a few simple areas that were critical in the attainment of larger organizational goals. In the words of John Rockart, CSFs are 'those few critical areas where things must go right for the business to flourish.' In the classic *Harvard Business Review* article 'Chief Executives Define Their Own Data Needs,' Rockart lists examples of CSFs (see Table 5.2).

Rockart's goals are essentially the same as our top-level market and financial goals, while his CSFs are similar to our BOS level measures. For example, 'styling' or 'quality dealer system' could be the key customer satisfaction measure, 'cost control' could be the key productivity measure (some CSFs, however, sound more like objectives, such as 'improved cost accounting'). In a sense, the middle level of our pyramid – customer satisfaction, flexibility, and productivity – is the critical success level. Like CSFs, each company will define different measures depending on their customer needs and internal strategies to meet those needs.

CSFs led to some improvement in performance measurement by helping executives to focus on a few key performance areas. Later,

Table 5.2 How attainment of organizational goals is supported by CSFs

Example	Goals	CSFs
For-profit concern	Earnings per share Return on investment Market share New product success	**Automotive industry** Styling Quality dealer system Cost control Meeting energy standards **Supermarket industry** Product mix Inventory Sales promotion Price
Non-profit concern	Excellence of health care Meeting needs of future health care environment	**Government hospital** Regional integration of health care with other hospitals Efficient use of scarce medical resources Improved cost accounting

Rockart and Christine V. Bullen, also of MIT's Center For Information Systems Research, added to the concept and uses of CSFs.[14] They cited three uses of CSFs:

1 To help an *individual manager* determine his or her information needs.
2 To aid an organization in its *general planning process* – for strategic, long range, and annual planning purposes.
3 To aid an organization in its *information systems* planning process.

They also introduced the notions of external and internal CSFs and hierarchical CSFs. There are some key differences between the CSFs of the 1970s and the newer yardsticks we advocate. Exhibit 5.2 depicts the major differences.

The growth of CSFs has led to the creation of new 'executive support systems.'[15] Powerful software packages are available today that allow executives to sit back in their chairs and look at key data presented as colorful graphs and drill down for additional detail with the mere click of a mouse or touch of the screen. For the most part these systems do not capture the kind of information necessary at the operating level to improve day-to-day decisions – although they certainly could do – as discussed in chapter 10.

Exhibit 5.2 CSFs and today's yardsticks

CSFs	New yardsticks
• not a performance measurement system	• a consistent set of criteria and a framework for measuring day-to-day operations
• addresses 'areas' of performance that are barometers of how the company will do	• day-to-day operational feedback for continuous improvement against business system as whole objectives
• critical to the success of an individual manager (vertical orientation)	• critical to the success of the business system (horizontal or customer orientation)
• interviews conducted with executives by 'outsider'	• interviews conducted by operating managers in the supplier–customer network, who are closer to the real-time decisions
• mostly high-level, executive audience	• information organized in a hierarchy to support all management levels in a consistent manner
• like MBO, manager- and individual-specific	• workflow- and customer-specific

As argued in chapter 2, executives need to do more than articulate a few areas where things must go right. Executives can gain better control of their company's future by implementing a consistent performance measurement system that extends down to department level.

Yardsticks must foster learning throughout the organization by continuously relating actions and measures to strategic objectives. A major change occurs when this happens. Focus shifts from 'managing by numbers' at the top, to continuous improvements in activities at business system level that provide competitive advantage. Thinking in terms of the business system emphasizes the need to work across functional boundaries. By taking a horizontal perspective on the workflows that deliver value to the customer (discussed in chapter 4), management are encouraged to think and act more as a team, both with respect to functions and with respect to issues of balancing customer satisfaction, flexibility, and productivity. As this perspective takes hold, it supplants the underlying logic of viewing organizations as a collection of separate functions.

With strategically tuned, customer-driven yardsticks, it becomes possible to translate strategic business objectives, both financial and non-financial, into operational measures that are readily understandable within the business system. This facilitates an *early warning system,* for corrective action when performance falters.

Critical success factors and corresponding measures are still powerful concepts. CSFs such as 'image in the financial markets,' 'reputation with customers,' and 'market success,' are just as important in the BOS. We just organized them differently and built a foundation for continuous and timely improvement. For example, the CSF 'inventory turns' at the BOS level is supported by on-time delivery and cycle time measures in each component of that business system. Another CSF, 'retention rate' in a diet and exercise company, is the result of how well quality and delivery expectations were met and at what price.

Figure 5.9 portrays several examples of the building blocks of success.

Bilingual managers

Dr Juran presents a pyramid of units of measure in his recent book *Juran on Planning for Quality.*[16] His pyramid (figure 5.10) portrays the relationship between corporate summaries and indices (primarily in the language of money) at the top level and operational units of measure for specific products and processes at the bottom level.

The top level of Juran's pyramid corresponds to the second level of the performance pyramid. However, the performance pyramid places equal weight on measures of market performance, such as market share, at the business unit level. This emphasis is essential especially in light of the Japanese demonstration that market share, rather than financial performance, is the critical performance indicator that ultimately leads to successful financial performance.

The second layer of Juran's pyramid is the translation layer from

Level
Business unit

Business operating system

Department

Measure
Market share

Customer satisfaction index

Percent meeting specification

Level
Business unit

Business operating system

Department

Measure
Market growth

Response time

On-time delivery, cycle time

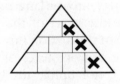

Level
Business unit

Business operating system

Department

Measure
Margins

Total factory productivity

Waste rate
(scrap, rework, inventory,
etc.)

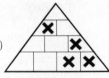

Level
Business unit

Business operating system

Department

Measure
Market share

Low costs (allows low price)

Cycle time, waste rate

Level
Business unit

Business operating system

Department

Measure
Return on assets

Inventory turns

Cycle time

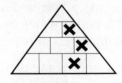

Figure 5.9   Building blocks of success: how measures are related

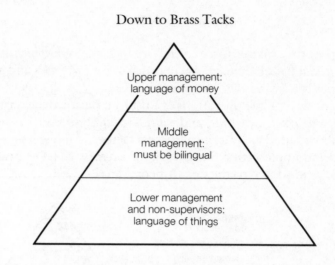

Figure 5.10   Common languages in the company

the corporate level to the department level. Juran states that the top layer of his pyramid is in the language of money for upper management. The next layer represents the language of middle management, which should be bilingual. They need to convert the language of money into the language of things for the troops, and the language of things into the language of money for upper management. It is not unlike the heart of the performance pyramid, which specifies the mode of translation through the three criteria of BOS performance.

The bottom level of Juran's pyramid reflects the language of things, not unlike the bottom level of the performance pyramid. Ideally the four criteria of day-to-day operating performance are made up of measures which are expressed in units rather than money.

Summary

Performance measures form a powerful management tool and can play a critical role in developing a firm's competitive advantage. To build a performance pyramid, or framework for evaluating operations, managers must:

- fully understand their organization's *vision* and *strategic objectives*
- foster *learning* in the organization by continually relating actions to strategic objectives
- give added emphasis to the *market-driven* side of the pyramid

- interpret the driving force in the organization (*customer satisfaction, flexibility,* or *productivity*) in order to set priorities and action agendas for day-to-day operations
- evaluate day-to-day operations against four performance criteria – *quality, delivery, cycle time,* and *waste* – *simultaneously*
- do more than identify 'critical success factors.' Managers must develop and implement a framework for a *consistent* set of measures that extends down to the departmental level.

Notes

1 George Stalk Jr, 'Time – The Next Source of Competitive Advantage,' *Harvard Business Review*, July–August 1988.
2 Stanley M. Davis, *Future Perfect* (Addison-Wesley, Reading, Mass., 1987).
3 Duncan McDougall, 'The Principle of Slack Ropes or Managing on Purpose,' *Operations Management Review*, Spring 1987.
4 Thomas E. Vollmann, Jeffrey Miller, and Alfred J. Nanni, 'Rethinking Manufacturing Equations with Just-In-Time' (Boston University Manufacturing Roundtable, 1986).
5 Richard G. Hamermesh, *Making Strategy Work* (John Wiley, New York, 1986).
6 Frederick W. Gluck, 'Vision and Leadership in Corporate Strategy,' *McKinsey Quarterly*, Winter 1981.
7 Kenneth Andrews, *The Concept of Corporate Strategy* (Dow Jones/Irwin, Homewood, Ill., 1971).
8 For a good treatment of the importance of market share measures, see: Robert D. Buzzelle and Bradley T. Gale, *The PIMS Principles* (Free Press, New York, 1987).
9 J. Robb Dixon, Alfred J. Nanni, and Thomas E. Vollmann, ' Breaking the Barriers: Measuring Performance for World Class Operations' (Boston University, 1989). This Manufacturing Research Report is based in part on the Manufacturing Futures Survey, an annual survey of companies conducted by Boston University in association with INSEAD in France and Wadesa University in Japan. This report contains an excellent discussion on the competitive dimensions of flexibility.
10 'How The New Math of Productivity Adds Up,' *Business Week*, June 6, 1988.
11 Davis, *Future Perfect*.
12 John F. Rockart, 'Chief Executives Define Their Own Data Needs,' *Harvard Business Review*, March–April 1979.

13 CSF was based on two earlier works: Ronald Daniel, 'Management Information Crisis,' *Harvard Business Review*, September–October 1961, and Robert Anthony, John Dearden, and Richard F. Vancil, *Management Control System* (Irwin, Homewood, Ill., 1972).

14 Christine V. Bullen and John F. Rockart, 'A Primer on Critical Success Factors,' Center for Information Systems Research, Working Paper no. 69 (Sloan School of Management, MIT, Cambridge, Mass., 1981). Also appears in *The Rise of Managerial Computing*, ed. J. F. Rockart and C. V. Bullen (Dow Jones/Irwin, Homewood, Ill., 1986).

15 Jeremy Main, 'At Last, Software CEOs Can Use,' *Fortune*, March 13, 1989.

16 J. M. Juran, *Juran on Planning for Quality* (Free Press, New York, 1988).

6

◇

Performance that Counts
to the Customer

◆

A customer is not dependent upon us. We are dependent on him.

Leon L. Bean, Founder, L.L. Bean & Co.

Lee Iacocca, chairman of the Chrysler Corporation, once said that the nine most important words in a company are: satisfy the customer, satisfy the customer, satisfy the customer. We could not agree more. In chapter 3 we emphasized the importance of strategy development in helping organizations understand who their customers are. In chapter 4 we provided a mapping technique to help you identify critical moments of truth with your customer. The importance of the market/customer side of the performance pyramid was underscored in chapter 5. Three different avenues all leading to the customer.

By now it should be obvious that the first thing a performance yardstick must do is give you feedback on how effectively your organization is providing value to the customer. In other words, are you doing the right things from the customer's perspective – and are you measuring what is important to them?

Unfortunately there are too many well-publicized stories about companies that thought they knew better than their customers. Japan's bolt from the blue in the automotive industry is a case in point. Customers demanded small, reliable cars with good mileage. Detroit thought otherwise and lost 30 percent of the marketplace. In the fast-paced world of computers, Wang Laboratories held on to its proprietary systems and minicomputer word-processing systems long after customers demanded industry standards and powerful professional computers. The result – lost market share and a lot of red ink.

On the pedestal

Measuring and reporting on customer satisfaction begins with the customer. After all, the customer is the reason your company exists. They deserve a place on the pedestal.

A customer's experience with your product or service is dictated by a simple formula, over which any company has a degree of control. The formula can be stated as:

$$CS = P - E$$

where CS is customer satisfaction, P is performance, and E is expectations. If customer satisfaction is equal to performance minus expectations, customers are happy when performance meets, or exceeds, expectations. Conversely, customers are unhappy when performance falls short of their expectations. Therefore, companies must pay attention not only to performance but to customer expectations as well.

Great expectations

John Young, president and CEO of Hewlett-Packard, recognizes the importance of setting and meeting expectations.

Satisfying customer needs and expectations is the number one reason for being in business. Customer responsiveness and loyalty to HP's products will ultimately determine the company's success or failure. And the standards by which customers judge HP's products have risen over the years. Failing to respond to these raised expectations is like denying the force of the tide.[1]

To some degree expectations can be managed. For example, many suppliers routinely negotiate with customers on delivery expectations although the goal is to eventually have customer request date and delivery date coincide. Once agreed to, those dates become key performance criteria.

Expectations are created by a number of specific mechanisms such as:

- advertising
- promises from a salesperson
- published specifications
- industry norms
- previous experience with the product or service
- experience with a competitor.

A severe imbalance between expectations and performance is usually devastating. For instance, many companies have unintentionally advertised more than their operations can deliver, which creates dissatisfied customers and loss of market share.

It is easy to understand why managing customer satisfaction is difficult in large organizations. Typically expectations are created way in advance of performance. Also, within most major corporations expectations are managed by one group of people and performance is managed by another. Managing expectations is in essence the marketing phase of executing business strategy. Performing to those expectations is the operations phase of existing business strategy (e.g. manufacturing, distribution, service). Since these functions are typically performed at different times and in many companies at different locations, sustained focus on customer satisfaction is difficult.

Expectations and performance are most likely to be synchronized at the conclusion of a strategic planning effort or at the introduction of a new product or service. On such occasions, the organization is more likely to have a clear, shared perception of the service or product offering and a unified commitment to carry out the offering as designed. Unfortunately, what starts out as a clear, unified vision built around the customer often degenerates over time into simply getting a department's job done. Why? The group responsible for managing expectations inevitably drifts apart from the group managing performance. At the same time, the customer's expectations are changing and evolving for a variety of reasons.

The BOS described in chapters 4 and 5 becomes the sensor device to help keep performance and expectations close together. Performance measures solidify the bond between provider and consumer. They provide:

- the monitoring tool to track and manage the expectations of the customer

- the means to communicate and translate those expectations into operational imperatives
- the feedback mechanism to show how well those expectations were met.

In other words, they indicate how closely the heat-seeking missile is zeroing in on the elusive expectations of the customer.

Apple of one's eye

While on-time delivery of high-quality product or service determines the performance side of the customer satisfaction equation, price, product, and service combine to determine the expectation variable in the formula.

A low price reduces expectations for the product or service. Conversely a high price raises expectations for the product or service. The $6,000 price tag on a Subaru or Escort does not merit the same set of expectations as that on a more expensive BMW or Mercedes.

While price is straightforward to both producer and consumer, it is important to distinguish and adequately define product and service. Product is easier to define. It is a physical unit. As such it has specific dimensions of quality. David Garvin describes these dimensions as:

1 *Performance* – the primary functionality or operating characteristics of the product
2 *Features* – secondary characteristics that supplement the basic functionality
3 *Reliability* – a reflection of the probability of failure within a specified time
4 *Conformance* – the degree to which a product's design and operating characteristics match pre-established standards
5 *Durability* – a measure of product life
6 *Serviceability* – the ease of repair
7 *Aesthetics* – how a product looks and feels
8 *Perceived quality* – overall impressions.[2]

In a service business the product may not be quite so tangible. More importantly in a service business, the product is the effective performance of a promise. For instance, a baggage handler in an airport promises to get your bags on the plane; a bank clerk promises to make change; a hotel reservation agent promises comfortable accommodation. As a product, the key measures are related to meeting expectations regarding the tangible attributes of the product or service and doing so reliably.

Fly in the ointment

A good product at a good price may not be enough to get or keep your customer. Service may be just as important to customer satisfaction as product and pricing. Service is an element of customer satisfaction which goes beyond the routine delivery of the company's basic products (or services). Customer service means all features, acts, and information that augment the customer's ability to realize the potential value of a core product or service.[3] For example, computer manufacturers sell more than hardware. What often distinguishes the good from the bad is the service provided: consultation on customized applications, training, maintenance, etc. In fact, the grand old names of industry are less and less industrial. A third of the revenues at General Electric and Borg-Warner, and half those at Westinghouse, come from services.[4]

The emphasis on customer service has not been restricted to the literature – it is of competitive advantage on the battlefield. Service has played a vital role in the success of Honda's Acura division. Likewise, American Express has succeeded to a great extent on the basis of customer service.

Even in the business-to-business marketplace expectations are growing for more service. Much of this is related to the movement toward JIT manufacturing. Companies are now attempting to use one good supplier, rather than buying solely on the basis of price from multiple suppliers. Benefits of JIT manufacturing come from the service aspect of the relationship between vendor and buyer.

In order for the vendor to supply the product as needed, the vendor must be able to:

- react quickly to fluctuations in demand
- provide 100 percent good product so that incoming inspection is not needed
- and in many instances, provide technical support and consultation regarding use of the product.

This consultation aspect of a JIT partnership becomes especially beneficial during the design and introduction of a new product. As two service experts put it: 'thanks to JIT, many business buyers and sellers have embraced the idea of co-destiny. They are planning future products and future capacity together and co-destiny is impossible without impeccable service.'[5]

Apple of discord

Dissatisfaction occurs when expectations are not met. In many respects, managing to avoid dissatisfaction is more important and more difficult than managing satisfaction. For example, in a dining experience at a restaurant, the price may be good, the product (the food) may be good, and the service overall may be good, but one incident could result in dissatisfaction. Incidents such as a bill which is incorrectly totaled, a coat stolen from the coat check room, or a dirty bathroom can create a dissatisfied customer. The same is true in big business. It is the 'little things' which may create the most dissatisfaction.

Customers let you know early when they are dissatisfied. In fact, there are warning signs of dissatisfaction. In their book *Customer Satisfaction*, Mack Hannan and Peter Karp characterize the warning signs of dissatisfaction in three categories: slowdown, putdown, and shutdown.[6]

Slowdown

Customer approval of your proposals comes more slowly. Projects that are approved may be stretched out or split up into several successive phases, each of which will require its own approval. The flow of customer data slows down.

Putdown

Access decreases to upper-level customer managers. Contacts are increasingly with lower functionaries. You can still get 'upstairs' but it happens less often and with less reward.

Shutdown

Plans for future work are shortened, becoming progressively shorter-term. It becomes difficult to open up discussions of migrations for your current work. The customer prefers to wait and see rather than plan and commit.

Unfortunately these warning signs are merely symptoms of an existing problem. They give no indication of the problem. Have customer expectations changed? Has performance slipped? Or both?

Awareness of and meticulous attention to the causes of dissatisfaction are key distinguishing attributes found in companies with superior customer service records.

One sure-fire way to keep customers happy is to pay attention to performance measurements important to them. Superior service companies enjoy reputations for distinctive service quality because they consistently meet their customers' expectations. Far from leaving anything to chance, they establish clear, customer-service-oriented performance standards throughout their organizations and then consistently and meticulously measure performance against those standards.

The common thread that runs through the measurement systems in the top service companies is that what counts is the customer's perception of the quality of service. Only the customer can determine whether performance has met their expectations.

Unfortunately not all companies are so meticulous about measuring customer satisfaction from the customer's perspective. Tom Peters and Nancy Austin, in their book *A Passion for Excellence,* describe a survey they made of 132 executives:

All 132 ranked long-term customer satisfaction first in importance. However, when asked how many of you measure any of your people directly on a third party or impartial quantitative in-house measure of long-term total customer satisfaction, the answer was 0.[7]

Another survey, conducted by the Forum Corporation, found similar gaps between promises and reality. Although many companies claim that customer satisfaction is important, less than one-third of the employees surveyed said that customer satisfaction was one of their organization's top three priorities.

External measurements are clearly needed in order to manage and understand expectations. In an article entitled 'Letting the Customer

Be the Judge of Quality,' Jeffrey Marr states:

external customer satisfaction measurement programs are not intended to replace internal measurements of quality, rather they should serve to augment the total quality assurance effort. The internal means are usually the fastest and best ways to know whether things are being done right. However to know whether you are doing the right things right, you must let the customer be the judge.[8]

To make sure they measure up to customer expectations, Analog Devices routinely monitors customer measures of company on-time delivery and quality performance. Internally generated measures are compared with the 'outside-in' view to make sure the trends are the same and performance standards are close.

Fit to a 'T'

Whether through customer focus groups, customer visits, surveys, or through new tools such as quality function deployment (QFD), companies that listen to their customers and understand their expectations and take action are gaining competitive advantage.

Customer focus groups

Companies such as IBM are changing long-standing practices of secrecy during product development. For example, during the design of its AS/400 minicomputer, IBM solicited users' opinions on the product and brought software companies into the planning process. After responding to customer criticisms, IBM launched the computer worldwide with more than 1,000 software applications available in 12 languages. In its first year the AS/400 sold 25,000 machines worth approximately $3 billion.[9] IBM's 'year of the customer' was more than an empty slogan.

To stay close to their customers, Rubbermaid's five divisions operate as autonomous companies. At the Little Tikes Company, a toy subsidiary, researchers watch through a two-way mirror at the company's employee day-care center to see which toys kids like best. In its housewares division, product developers listen to customer focus groups. One example shows how the company skips test marketing and gives customers what they want: when focus group participants complained of puddles in their dish trays, designers quickly answered by increasing the height of the drain tray a bit at the back, to help water flow into the sink.[10]

It is important to note in both the IBM and Rubbermaid examples that new product introduction (formally a backroom function) is arguably the most critical operating system in terms of customer satisfaction.

Customer visits

Another mechanism to stay close to your customer is customer visits. To get a jump on the competition, Allegheny Ludlum Corporation, the largest producer of specialty steel in the US, regularly sends development teams to visit customers. There they talk with engineers to find out what is needed. Again, an example shows the fruits of their attention. After visiting a convention of companies that made heating equipment, they learned of concerns about meeting impending heat efficiency laws. Allegheny Ludlum researchers quickly scoured their patents for a corrosion-resistant alloy to help reduce heat loss. They found one and began marketing a product three years before the law was passed.[11]

Surveys

Surveys are yet another simple method of listening to the voice of the customer. Marriott, the hotel chain, regularly polls its top customers to find out what it is doing right and what it is doing wrong. Marriott uses two kinds of polls: (1) regular scientific, third-party sampling and surveying, and (2) a less formal, more open guest satisfaction index. The guest satisfaction index is compiled from in-room survey forms and therefore comes in frequently. It is used as a rolling indicator of how well a property is satisfying the guests and is taken as seriously as the more scientific monthly telephone surveys.[12]

QFD

Other successful companies, such as Hewlett-Packard, ITT, and Ford Motor Company, are using new tools to design products and services to meet customer expectations. One such tool is quality function deployment (QFD). Originating in Japan, QFD is a system for designing product or service based on customer wants, involving all members of the supplying organization.[13] As such it is a conceptual map for interfunctional planning and communications. Two QFD experts describe the tool thus:

A set of planning and communication routines, quality function deployment focuses and coordinates skills within an organization, first to design, then to manufacture and market goods that customers want to purchase and will continue to purchase. The foundation of [QFD] is the belief that products should be designed to reflect customers' desires and tastes – so marketing people, design engineers, manufacturing staff must work closely together from the time a product is first conceived.[14]

Companies utilizing a QFD approach are benefiting in several, measurable ways:

- higher sales because customers are getting what they want (quality) when they need it (delivery)
- faster design time
- reduction in waste as a result of fewer engineering changes.

Common to each of these tools is the fact that they are designed to track customer expectations.

Quality and delivery: performance pillars revisited

High-quality products or services (based on customer-driven target values) and regular on-time delivery are the performance pillars of customer satisfaction. While global measures such as product ratings or number of complaints are important indices, they do not translate directly into operational actions to correct a problem. Day-to-day measures are needed to help managers control a process.

Quality

In chapter 5 we defined quality as 'meeting customer expectations… 100% of the time.' Dr Juran maintains that this is achievable through the delivery of defect-free product or service. Armand V. Fiegenbaum, the father of total quality control, elaborates on what this means:

Quality is a customer determination, not an engineer's determination, not a marketing determination or a general management determination. It is based upon the customer's actual experience with the product or service, measured against his or her requirements – stated or unstated, conscious or merely sensed, technically operational or entirely subjective – and always represents a moving target in a competitive market.[15]

This definition takes an outside-in view of your company. It does not matter what you think your quality is. Your marketplace customer's opinion is what counts. But how do you translate customer feedback upstream in your organization? Once inside your organization, interpreting the marketplace signals and acting on them often turns into the business equivalent of the Tower of Babel. Without a common understanding of quality and synchronized operations there is little chance that the end results will be achieved.

The BOS concept introduced in chapters 4 and 5 is a tool that enables you to synchronize your operations around a common purpose. New requirements from the marketplace customer and changing priorities are quickly communicated as quality and delivery demands from the downstream departments. Stan Davis, author of *Future Perfect*, warns against the tendency to view other employees as 'internal customers.' To him there is only one customer – the customer in the marketplace. His concern is well noted. Employees who think of other employees as their customer *may* lose sight of the business in favor of the organization.[16]

In our approach to changing performance yardsticks, we guard against that pitfall by starting the measurement process in the department furthest downstream. As detailed in chapters 8 and 9, feedback should flow upstream to make sure every department in the BOS stays in touch with the end-user. When all employees in an internal supplier–customer network are focused on the performance of the BOS as a whole, the end-user or marketplace customer's expectations are more likely to be met. This approach has profound implications on how quality is measured within companies.

- Quality must be measured from the downstream department's perspective since they are closer to the end-customer regardless of political boundaries and egos.
- Measures of quality that are self-aggrandizing and ignore the downstream customer's needs are the worst measures of all because they motivate the wrong behavior.
- Some companies think that measuring 'first pass yield' at a process step is a quality measure. But it really is not. It is a waste measure.

The percentage that did not pass the first time must be reworked or scrapped. It only becomes poor quality if the reject is passed downstream.

- Quality of service provided may be just as important as a physical product passed downstream.
- Since everyone is a part of the BOS and has a customer, quality is everyone's job – not just that of the quality control department.
- The quality of the entire process is reflected in the last department in the BOS. This measure should be the most watched barometer in the system.
- For many companies, the new definition of quality represents a new challenge. Usher it in with a total quality management program. But don't stop at creating an 'awareness.' Get quality improvement efforts started throughout the organization. These efforts need to be developed at grassroots level on a project-by-project basis and sustained through a consistent set of measures.

Delivery

In chapter 5, we introduced delivery as the second pillar of customer satisfaction. Good products or services are only of value to the customer once they take delivery. Sometimes companies confuse quality and delivery measures. For example, one company we worked with defined on-time delivery as the percentage meeting customer due date. If the order was wrong or incomplete they marked that against their quality performance. Our definition of delivery suggests that late delivery would include incorrect shipments and incomplete shipments as well as late shipments. Poor quality from the customer's perspective would result from the product or service not meeting expectations (did not work, failed to solve a problem, etc.) This definition of delivery has some major ramifications for companies:

- Schedules become contracts. Late delivery in an upstream department not only increases the risk of late delivery to the customer but adds waste in the downstream operations (idle equipment, more inventory, etc.)
- Customers buy whole products and services; everything must be on time.
- Rush orders should be measured separately. This is similar to a vendor charging more for 'rush orders.'

- Delivery expectations dictate workflow principles and cycle time goals.
- Delivery is a source of additional profits for customers.
- As customers get closer to the producer, the delivery cycle shrinks.
- JIT demands routine on-time delivery. Missed deliveries will cost both supplier and customer.
- In a JIT environment, early delivery is judged as missed delivery. On time means on the promised day – not earlier or later.
- Delivery date is more than a promise, when it is guaranteed.

Summary

The first thing a performance yardstick must do is give you feedback on how effectively your organization is providing value to the customer. In other words, are you doing the right things from the customer's perspective?

- Measure what is important to your customer.
- Put your customers on a pedestal – but do not be afraid to talk to them. Listen to your customers and turn their expectations into operating imperatives.
- Remember to manage expectations. Your promises, whether through advertising or sales pitches, set the customer's expectations.
- Use quality and delivery performance measures to solidify the bond between producer and consumer.
- Pay attention to product, price, and service. Do not let service be the fly in the ointment.
- Don't just talk about quality. Do something about it. Implement a top down total quality management program. It does not matter whether you call it TQM, TQC, or QIP (quality improvement program) – a rose by any other name smells as sweet.
- Stay close to your customer; techniques such as focused groups, QFD, or customer visits will help.
- Measures of quality that are self-aggrandizing and ignore the downstream customer's needs are the worst measures of all because they motivate the wrong behavior.
- Since everyone is a part of the BOS and has a customer, quality is everyone's job – not just that of the quality control department.

- Good products or services are only of value to the customer once they take delivery. 'On time' means that the product or service was not late, it was complete, and consisted of the right items.
- On-time delivery requires adherence to schedules in the BOS.
- JIT is changing the expectations concerning delivery. As JIT takes hold in more and more industries, on-time delivery will become an expectation with no exceptions.

Notes

1   John A. Young, 'The Quality Focus at Hewlett-Packard,' *Journal of Business Strategy*, Spring 1985.
2   David A. Garvin, *Managing Quality* (Free Press, New York, 1988).
3   William H. Davidow and Bro Uttal, *Total Customer Service: The Ultimate Weapon* (Harper & Row, New York, 1989).
4   Stanley M. Davis, *Future Perfect* (Addison-Wesley, Reading, Mass., 1987).
5   Davidow and Uttal, *Total Customer Service*.
6   Mack Hannan and Peter Karp, *Customer Satisfaction: How to Maximize, Measure and Market Your Company's Ultimate Product* (AMACON, New York, 1989).
7   Thomas J. Peters and Nancy K. Austin, *A Passion for Excellence* (Random House, New York, 1989).
8   Jeffrey Marr, 'Letting the Customer Be the Judge of Quality,' *Quality Progress*, October 1986.
9   'IBM,' *Fortune*, August 14, 1989.
10 'Masters of Innovation,' *Business Week*, April 10, 1989.
11 Ibid.
12 Ron Zemke and Dick Schaaf, *The Service Edge* (New American Library, New York, 1989).
13 Bob King, *Better Designs in Half the Time* (GOAL/QPC, Methuen, Mass., 1987).
14 John R. Hauser and Don Clausing, 'The House of Quality,' *Harvard Business Review*, May-June, 1988.
15 A.V. Fiegenbaum, *Total Quality Control* (McGraw-Hill, New York, 1983).
16 Davis, *Future Perfect*.

7

◇

Performance that Counts to the Bottom Line

◆

Figures on productivity in the US do not help to improve productivity in the US. Measures of productivity are like statistics on accidents: they tell you all about the number of accidents in the home, on the road, and at the work place, but they do not tell you how to reduce the frequency of accidents.

W. Edwards Deming

If the new yardsticks are to help companies focus on doing the right things, they must also help them to do them well. Satisfying the customer, as described in chapter 6, gets you off on the right foot. But if your company is a for-profit organization, you must be concerned about profit maximization. Note that we said profit maximization and not cost reduction. As Wickham Skinner put it, 'an obsession with cost reduction produces a narrowness of vision and an organizational backlash that works against the purpose of the organization.'[1]

The new math of productivity

Productivity has been the most watched and measured performance criterion since the days of Frederick Taylor. Even today, productivity still commands the front page of business journals and is usually a hot topic with government and industry leaders alike. In fact, productivity may be overemphasized at the expense of customer satisfaction and longer-term market goals. Still, productivity measures dominate company scorecards: dollars per square foot in retail businesses, output per person in manufacturing companies, total factor productivity in a production facility, and so on. While there is nothing wrong with these measures, there are serious problems in the way they get translated into day-to-day operations. For example, global productivity measures are systemic in nature, yet local productivity measures, such as spending variances, performance to budget, and purchase price variance, are reported in a vacuum.

In today's economy, productivity is all about managing time effectively and eliminating waste. Emphasis on waste reduction and faster cycle times at the local department level improves productivity in the BOS which, in turn, improves cash flow, return on investment, and net profitability.

Time is money

Time, as a component of flexibility, is being touted as the next competitive advantage by consultants and researchers alike. Why is time getting so much attention? Vigorous global competition, product proliferation, and advanced technologies have led to shorter product lifecycles. How quickly companies can translate customer needs to product determines both the amount of capital invested and the sales and profit curve in the marketplace. As illustrated in figure 7.1a, the longer the product stays in development, the more that capital is tied up — pushing out the break-even point (BE1 to BE2). A break-even point further to the right means lower market share, tighter profit margins, and poor return on investments.

A 1983 McKinsey & Company study also confirms the significance of time-to-market. Shipping six months late results in over 30 percent reduction in profits in high growth companies, while a 50 percent development cost overrun only reduced profits by 5 percent as illustrated in figure 7.1b.

Cycle time can be defined as:

$$\text{process time} + \text{inspection time} + \text{move time} + \text{queue time} + \text{storage time}$$

Many companies in both manufacturing and service industries are piloting projects to reduce iterations, simplify workflows, eliminate unnecessary steps and movement, eliminate bottlenecks, and reduce

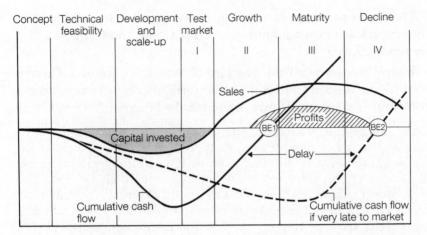

Figure 7.1(a)   Fast cycle benefits: get to market early to maximize sales and profits (adapted from D. Bruce Merrifield, 'Industrial Survival via Management Technology,' *Journal of Business Strategy*)

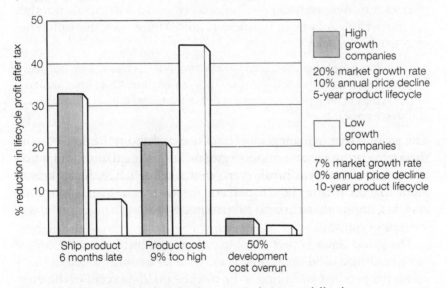

Figure 7.1(b)   New product development and commercialization
Source: McKinsey & Company

delays all in the name of reduced cycle time. For example, at Caterpillar's Decatur plant, a motor-grade front axle used to travel 300 miles in the assembly process. After a cellular manufacturing design was introduced, the sub-assembly moved only a few hundred feet and total cycle time dropped from 90 days to 8 hours.

These companies emphasize cycle time because it is within their control, it has a powerful influence on flexibility, and a major effect on productivity.

Joseph Bower from the Harvard Business School and Thomas Hout of the Boston Consulting Group articulate how fast cycle times contribute to better performance across the board:

Costs drop because production materials and information collect less overhead and do not accumulate as work-in-process inventory. Customer service improves because the lead time from order receipt to shipment diminishes. Quality is higher because you cannot speed up the production cycle overall unless everything is done right the first time. Innovation becomes a characteristic behavior pattern because rapid new product development cycles keep the company in close touch with customers and their needs.[2]

Of course, there is a difference between time and speed. Speed implies that things seem fast or slow, according to whether or not they are in rhythm. A famous Japanese Kendo Master saw this difference over 300 years ago:

Very skillful people can manage a fast rhythm, but it is bad to beat hurriedly. If you try to beat too quickly you will get out of time. Of course, slowness is bad. Really skillful people never get out of time, and are always deliberate, and never appear busy.[3]

The point is that managers must be concerned about the flow of work throughout the entire business system. To make quantum improvements in time, such as cutting time-to-market in half, reducing manufacturing cycle time by 75 percent, or cutting a loan application review from weeks to hours, often requires radical changes in the way work is organized.

The good news is that these gains are achievable because only 5 percent of the total cycle time is devoted to adding value! In many cases, the product is waiting to be worked on 95 percent of the time. The same is true for paper transactions. There is a lot of opportunity for improvement and much can be done by focusing on cycle time.

Unnecessarily long cycle time contributes directly to poor strategic performance regarding productivity and flexibility. For example, in production, rapid cycle time will minimize work-in-progress inventory and should eliminate or at least minimize the need for finished goods inventories. Carrying costs will be reduced and cash flow improved. Also, the cost of reworking work-in-process and finished goods to comply with an engineering change order for a specific customer requirement is eliminated. Productivity is enhanced by the rapid identification and correction of problems before too many defective sub-assemblies and/or finished products are built. Rapid cycle time means that emphasis is placed on building the product or delivering the service right the first time. As the build cycle shrinks, it becomes more predictable and dependable. By reducing the distance (time) between consumer and producer, customer satisfaction improves. It is important to note that it is the behind the scenes functions (such as manufacturing and new product introduction) where cycle time has received less focus. In service delivery operations where the customer waits for delivery, cycle time has always been a consideration. Examples are found in restaurants, 24-hour photo labs, dry cleaners, etc.

Waste not, want not

We have defined productivity in terms of managing activities efficiently (i.e. doing the right things well). Therefore, unproductive activity can be thought of as the non-value-added resources, or *waste*, incurred in meeting the requirements of the customer. Waste includes all the costs associated with failures, appraisals, and surpluses.

'Pure waste' consists of those activities and expenses that are totally unnecessary, such as scrap rework and useless 'bells and whistles' on equipment. 'Hidden waste' comprises operations without value added, such as kitting, incoming inspection, and warranty repair, that are necessary because of poor operating conditions.[4]

Waste has been tolerated in some instances because it is built into the standard cost system. For example, a Western Massachusetts paper company builds a 30 percent waste factor into its standard. Oddly enough, the term for waste in the paper industry is 'broke.' As one engineer put it to us: 'with a 30 percent broke standard, the company will be broke in a few years.'

Everybody knows that waste is bad, yet curiously there is often a love–hate relationship. For example, excess inventory, appraisal, and failure costs are clearly wasteful activities, as are the costs of processing waste, such as the preparation of scrap reports. Yet these activities create jobs: accountants count the inventory and prepare reports; incoming inspectors test the material; and the repair department fixes the failures. Elimination of waste also means the elimination of these jobs.

Specific examples of waste found in various organizations would include: scrap, rework, work-in-process, vendor defects, internal failures, accidents, absenteeism, incoming inspection, purges, warranty costs, tests, etc.).

Sometimes it is difficult to sift out the waste from the worthwhile. Prevention costs, such as vision machines at the front of the process, vendor engineering for ship-to-stock, preventive maintenance on equipment, are examples of value-added spending but often are the first candidates for elimination in belt-tightening times.

Knowing the ropes

The Japanese have had the most experience with JIT, which some have defined in terms of continuous improvement (*kaizen* in Japanese) and the elimination of waste (or *muda* in Japanese). They

Table 7.1   Canon's nine waste categories

Waste category	Nature of waste	Type of economization
Work-in-process	Stocking items not immediately needed	Inventory improvement
Rejection	Producing defective products	Fewer rejects
Facilities	Having idle machinery and breakdowns, taking too long for set-up	Increase in capacity utilization ratio
Expenses	Overinvesting for required output	Curtailment of expenses
Indirect labour	Excess personnel due to bad indirect labor system	Efficient job assignment
Design	Producing products with more functions than necessary	Cost reduction
Talent	Employing people for jobs that can be mechanized or assigned to less-skilled people	Labor saving or labor maximization
Motion	Not working according to work standard	Improvement of work standard
New-product run-up	Making a slow start in stabilizing the production of a new product	Faster shift to full line production

Source: Massaki Imai, *Kaizen: The Key to Japan's Competitive Success* (Random House, New York, 1986).

have recognized a simple fact: before you can eliminate waste you must find it. Table 7.1 shows how Canon categorizes waste. It provides a framework for identifying waste often buried in daily operations.

Canon's list is not the only way to categorize waste. Toyota uses the grouping shown in exhibit 7.1.

Exhibit 7.1   Toyota's seven wastes

Waste in processing
Waste of time
Waste in making defective parts
Waste of motion
Waste of overproduction
Waste of inventory
Waste of movement

Source: Quality Progress, April 1988.

Companies in deep trouble have difficulty in distinguishing between value-added and non-value-added activities. Companies on the verge of disaster can probably quantify the problem but are paralyzed by its magnitude. Successful companies, such as Toyota, Honda, Canon, 3M, Analog Devices, etc., involve everyone in the solution. For example, at the Honda Maryville plant, 2,000 safety and 10,000 quality improvements were implemented in 1988 alone.

Cost of quality

Our treatment of waste is similar to Crosby's 'cost of quality.'[5] We agree with Crosby that quality is actually free and waste is the expensive and unnecessary culprit. We differ, however, over the kinds of costs identified and quantified.

'Cost-of-quality' programs typically categorize costs in four areas:

1 prevention costs
2 appraisal or detection costs
3 internal failure costs
4 external failure costs.

By our definition, 'prevention' spending is not waste. We do not want to penalize managers for moving quality upstream in the process.

Typically, 'cost of quality' is calculated at a high level, such as a plant, business unit, or the company as a whole. The reporting of this data can lead the unwary into some of the traps of financial reporting, so that operating information is:

- translated into financial data
- after the fact
- too aggregated to be useful to line managers.

Others have noted inherent limitations in 'cost-of-quality'-type reporting:

- Quality cost measurement does not solve quality problems.
- Quality cost reports do not suggest specific action.
- Quality costs are susceptible to short-term mismanagement.
- It is difficult to match effort and accomplishment.
- Important costs may be omitted (i.e improvement in yields may postpone the need for a costly new facility).
- Inappropriate costs may be included in quality cost reports.
- Many quality costs are susceptible to measurement errors.[6]

To some extent, all performance measures run these risks. We advocate reporting waste in operational terms as frequently as possible for corrective action. To help focus on corrective action reporting waste dollar amount is not enough. We recommend that a Pareto-type analysis of the components of waste (e.g. inventory, rework may make up 80 percent of the reported dollars). We have included specific guidelines in chapter 8.

To know beans

Where are the bean counters in all of this? After all, the traditional goals of cost accounting have been to provide:

1 proper *inventory valuation* based on generally accepted accounting practices
2 *strategic information* related to product line profitability, pricing, and make-versus-buy
3 *performance measures* for operational control.

For the past 50 years or so, accountants have focused almost exclusively on inventory valuation – getting information right for the financial statements. In the US, the Securities Exchange Commission Act 1933 caused a shift from *management accounting* to *cost accounting*. New specialties were created in the areas of debt/equity structuring, reporting of financial data to the stockholder, and auditing.

For much of the past 50 years, it was assumed the standard accounting model provided good information on product cost and variances were a good way to evaluate operational performance. While that may have been true prior to the Second World War, it is no longer valid today.[7] Robin Cooper and Bob Kaplan summarize the problem this way:

distorted cost information is the result of sensible accounting choices made decades ago, when most companies manufactured a narrow range of products. Back then, the costs of direct labor and materials, the most important production factors, could be traced easily to individual products . . . Today, product lines and marketing channels have proliferated. Direct labor now represents a small fraction of corporate costs, while expenses covering factory support operations, marketing, distribution, engineering and other overheads have exploded.[8]

Product cost: chicken or egg?

Accountants are awakening to a new challenge: to provide strategic cost information – concerning pricing, sourcing, product design, and continuous improvement – in addition to their role of cost controllers. Leading the way to 'relevance found' is activity accounting. CAM–I defines activity accounting as: 'the collection of financial and operating performance information about significant activities of the business.'[9] Activity accounting is concerned with the factors that create cost and determine future spending. Some have used this concept to provide better information on product cost. Most notably, Cooper and Kaplan from the Harvard Business School have coined the term 'activity-based costing.' This term captures the essence of the tie between costs and the activities that cause those costs. Essentially, activity accounting reflects a change in thinking from 'individual products consume costs or resources' to 'products consume activities and activities consume resources.'[10] Overhead costs are 'allocated' on the basis of a 'bill of activity' rather than on a volume basis. For each activity, a number of causal factors or cost drivers can be identified. Table 7.2 depicts several major cost drivers in a typical manufacturing company.

Table 7.2   Activity accounting

Activity	Cost driver
Scheduling	Number of production schedule changes
Purchasing	Number of vendors
Incoming inspection	Number of parts not on ship-to-stock
Setting up a machine	Set-up time
Assembly	Number of parts
Rework	Number of engineering change orders

In a sense, cost drivers are really performance measures. Given that the overriding objective of strategic cost information is to provide relevant, timely information to support decision-making, it makes sense to keep the information in operational terms in manufacturing: quality, delivery, cycle time, and waste. The translation of these output measures into existing product cost data will happen after the fact and, like so many of the traditional cost accounting variances, must be unbundled and translated back into operational directives. After all, what information sends the clearer message:

product *X* really costs 10 percent more

or

design with fewer parts; get more parts on ship-to-stock;
reduce cycle time; lower in-process scrap?

While the latter is more direct and action-oriented, both pieces of information are critical to management. However the who, what, where, when, and why differ somewhat. Exhibit 7.2 depicts some of the major differences between activity-based costing and the new performance yardsticks.

Exhibit 7.2 Some differences between activity-based costing and performance yardsticks

Activity-based costing	The new yardsticks
• Product cost model	• Performance yardsticks
• Cost drivers	• Performance indicators
• Primarily deals with cost, indirect treatment of quality and flexibility	• Quantifies customer satisfaction, flexibility, and productivity
• Factory focus	• Used in any business system
• Feedback (manufacturing costs) relevant to other business systems (design)	• Feedback germane to supplier–customer network within the business system

---

Motivation should be in the form of operating signals provided by the performance yardsticks. The hook to activity-based costing is in the word 'activity.' Managers driven to reduce cycle time and eliminate waste view operations as the management of activities, not costs. Consistently reinforced measures should help all employees to focus on those areas where performance will translate into higher productivity. Accountants can then use this same activity-related information as the basis for the budget process and product cost. But the latter is more of a backroom exercise to produce a more relevant cost model. In this way, the cost accounting model reflects the new operating environment rather than forcing operations to fit a model from the roaring twenties!

As discussed in chapter 10, activity-based costing can be a powerful tool when applied in the new product introduction process. If used to set target costs, activity-based costing provides both strategic pricing information and immediate feedback before actual costs are committed. In this sense, it is a cost prevention tool.

Flogging a dead horse

The passion for reporting traditional variances may be a difficult behavior to overcome. As noted in table 2.2, the traditional cost accounting variances motivate the wrong actions if used for anything but adjusting inventory.

- Purchase price variance motivates the buyer to increase order quantities to get the best price, often ignoring the quality and delivery requirements of the department that transforms those parts into product. The net result is often mythical cost savings in procurement and real excess inventory and inspection costs for production.
- Machine utilization variance motivates the worker in a particular workcell to produce more parts than required (and often the wrong parts for future consumption).
- The scrap component in the standard cost model results in built-in waste. Managers are not encouraged to eliminate waste unless it exceeds the standard.
- Absorption variances motivate managers to produce excess inventory to absorb more expenses.

Spending variances also have a tendency to be misused. Budget variances are related to a plan and not to performance. In the new productivity context, cost is viewed in terms of the excess money (or effort) spent in order to achieve the required quality, delivery, and process time objectives. At the business system level, the main objective is to improve productivity by reducing overall costs. For example, a factory objective is to lower the ratio of cost/output. At the department level, cost is reported in terms of waste. A strong focus on eliminating waste at the department level is directly connected to the factory's overall cost performance. Productivity improvement or value engineering activities are targeted at departments with significant waste and not at those departments with 'unfavorable spending variances.'

What is good for the goose may kill the gander

External financial reporting and internal operational control represent two fundamentally different functions. The former is guided by generally accepted accounting principles, tax laws, and the needs of stockholders. Operational control, on the other hand, is guided by strategy, impact on the bottom line, and how well customer expectations are met. Both functions are necessary for the success of the company, but how well the needs of each are being met must be measured in different ways. Clearly, reporting done only for the benefit of the stockholder can have a devastating long-term impact on a company's performance. However, completely severing the link between the external financial numbers and the day-to-day operating metrics may be an overreaction to the problem.

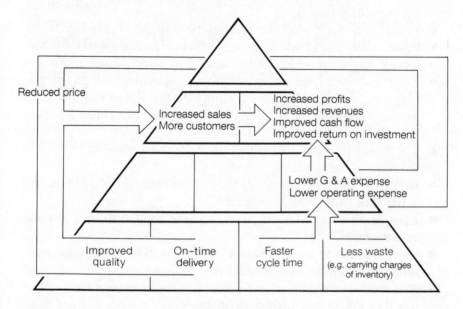

Figure 7.2   The new yardstick and the bottom line

The new yardstick is formed under a simple assumption: fast cycle time and elimination of waste improves productivity, which improves financial performance. Figure 7.2 shows some of the relationships between the local operating measures and the financial results. Longitudinal studies at several firms are beginning to verify the assumption. For example, companies that achieve fast cycle times are reporting triple the revenue growth and double the profits over industry-average competitors.[11]

Summary

Managing to the bottom line is an old saying, but it carries a new meaning in today's world economy. Productivity is all about managing time more effectively and eliminating waste in the pursuit of meeting customer expectations. Some changes in mindset for the accountant and operating manager alike are necessary.

- Think profit maximization, not cost reduction.
- Reducing cycle time in all aspects of the company's operations is a competitive necessity.
- Systematic changes are required in the way time is managed.
- Faster cycle times lead to lower product costs, improved customer service, higher product quality, and more timely innovations.
- Time and speed are not synonymous. Speeding things up may only mean doing the wrong things faster. The objective is to increase the pace or flow of work through the entire business system.
- To eliminate waste, managers must learn to separate the waste from the worthwhile.
- Rewards should be given to those who know how to eliminate waste, not those who manage it.
- Everybody should be involved in waste reduction, not just the acccountant.
- The fastest way to motivate corrective action is through non-financial measures, not product cost information.
- Better cost information and better yardsticks are not the same – but they do complement each other.
- Stop flogging a dead horse. Accounting variances have been inappropriate for decades!
- Fast cycle times and the elimination of waste will equal better financial performance. This is not just wishful thinking. Companies such as Honda and Benetton have reported growth rates over three times the industry average and double the profitability.

Notes

1 Wickham Skinner, 'The Productivity Paradox,' *Harvard Business Review*, July–August 1986.
2 Joseph L. Bower and Thomas M. Hout, 'Fast-Cycle Capability for Competitive Power,' *Harvard Business Review*, November–December 1988.
3 Miyamoto Mushasi, *A Book of Five Rings* (Overlook Press, Woodstock, NY, 1974).

4 Yasuhiro Monden, *Toyota Production System* (Productivity Press Inc.,
   Cambridge, Mass., 1988).
5 Philip B. Crosby, *Quality is Free* (Mentor, New York, 1979).
6 Wayne J. Morse, Harold P. Roth, and Kay M. Poston, *Measuring, Planning, and Controlling Costs* (National Association of Accountants,
   Montvale, NJ, 1987).
7 H. Thomas Johnson and Robert S. Kaplan, *Relevance Lost: The Rise and
   Fall of Management Accounting* (Harvard Business School Press, Boston, Mass., 1987).
8 Robin Cooper and Robert S. Kaplan, 'Measure Costs Right: Make the
   Right Decisions,' *Harvard Business Review*, September–October 1988.
9 Callie Berliner and James A. Brimson, eds, *Cost Management for Today's
   Advanced Manufacturing* (Harvard Business School Press, Boston,
   Mass., 1988).
10 Peter B. B. Turney, 'Using Activity-Based Costing to Achieve Manufac-
    turing Excellence,' *Journal of Cost Management*, Summer 1989.
11 Time-Based Competition Conference, Sponsored by the Operations
    Roundtable (Vanderbilt University, Nashville, Tenn.).

8

◇

Custom Tailoring Performance Measures

◆

One pound of learning takes ten pounds of common sense to apply it.

A crisis such as lost market share or disappointing earnings (or real disappointing losses) usually gets top management thinking about performance measures. The yardsticks are examined closely and measures are questioned. A typical management response is to create a taskforce to seek out new measures that will provide clues as to what went wrong. All too often, a quick fix is sought through a laundry list of 'critical success factors' and slight improvements are made. The taskforce fades away and the troops return to business as usual. But it was 'business as usual' that got the company into trouble in the first place.

Getting started

This chapter provides the tools needed to build a world-class performance measurement system. The first step for management is to get to grips with their business priorities and to clearly communicate those priorities to operations. An effective measurement system starts with clear top-down direction.

The rest of the chapter describes the process for building a dynamic measurement system from the bottom up. Worksheets, questionnaires, and guidelines are provided for:

- probing for critical performance measurement issues
- profiling and critiqueing existing performance indicators
- defining customer satisfaction measures

- developing internal productivity measures
- compiling key indices, where appropriate
- designing an effective scorecard
- tailoring information to support decisions.

A beacon in the night

Prior to developing indicators of performance for departments within a BOS, it is essential that the priorities of the BOS as a whole be understood and made explicit to each department within the BOS.

Typically BOS priorities are implicit rather than explicit. People may think that they know what those priorities are. The tone of a management memo, an unexpected visit from a vice-president, or a new management initiative may provide some clues. As noted in chapter 2, more often than not, these signals emanate from functional silos or from outdated performance indicators. When two or more different priorities reach the operating level, confusion supplants direction. Chaos thrives.

Developing the priorities of a BOS from scratch is beyond the scope of this book. Understanding those priorities is not. Developing and defining the priorities of a BOS falls into the realm of strategic planning and management. As discussed in chapter 3 and, especially, chapter 5, the priorities (and goals) of a BOS are driven by the corporate vision and goals for the business as a whole. If there is no direction, or tangible objectives at either the business or the BOS level, effort is best spent on clearing up the ambiguity by developing a strategic plan.

Once those strategies are developed, management must translate them into operational priorities. Clear direction is critical when market conditions change (or industries mature), strategies change, priorities shift, or one aspect of performance needs particular attention.

For instance, for many computer companies, the nature of the business changed dramatically from a seller's market to a buyer's market. As a result, Data General, Prime, Unisys, DEC, and Wang Laboratories are busy restructuring their companies for survival. As new strategies emerge, the priorities for each business system change. For example, in the order-to-delivery process for computers, the priority is changing from delivery (where anything that could be made could be sold) to reduced cycle times (where the product would not be made unless it was sold). This change in emphasis from growth to profitability has been a major culture shock!

Typically managers believe that they are clear about their strategies and priorities. Unfortunately, stating the strategies and priorities is one thing, obtaining a common understanding and commitment to them is another. Failure to get the message across frustrates top management and bewilders the troops. While this may seem paradoxical in the 'information age,' the problem often boils down to conflicting signals – especially in periods of transition.

The next section describes a proven process for filtering these signals and providing the guiding light for the BOS. A beacon from senior management is a welcome sign to the ships lost in a sea of chaos.

Priority no. 1: understanding your priorities

Three major driving forces behind the business system need to be clarified: customer satisfaction, flexibility, and productivity. All three may be present but at different levels of intensity. One should be dominant. *By understanding the driving force of the business operating system, it becomes easier to identify priorities at the department level.* The worksheet shown in figure 8.1 can be used to reach consensus about the priorities of the business system.

If a department supports more than one BOS (e.g. a fabrication shop supports both R&D prototypes for new product introduction and production's need for product) each BOS should be considered separately (see Business I and Business II columns). At this stage the emphasis should be on BOS priorities, not the department's priorities. Department priority may differ as a result of improvement needs, or when the downstream customer influences a specific priority for performance which will enhance overall BOS performance.

Each manager in the BOS should complete the form. Managers should indicate what the current priorities are believed to be (as reflected in actual operating behavior) by distributing 100 points down the 'is' column. Similarly, managers distribute 100 points down the 'should be' column, identifying any desired changes in priorities. Two analyses are important:

- the degree of convergence or divergence among the different functions

- the size of the gap between 'is' and 'should be.'

Agreement on priorities across different functions within the business system must be obtained to prevent conflicting signals. Priorities must also be made explicit to each level in the organization.

Department: _____ Date: _____				
Priority description	Business I		Business II	
	Is	Should be	Is	Should be
1 Produce and deliver products/services at the *lowest possible cost*				
2 Produce and deliver products/services at consistent levels of *quality and reliability* that are both significantly higher than the competition and are recognized by customers				
3 Meet unexpected changes in customer requirements that call for *short delivery cycles*				
4 Meet promised *delivery commitments* consistently over long periods of time				
5 Contribute to higher return on investment through *asset management*				
6 Respond quickly to required significant *changes in volume* of activity (up or down) . . . capacity				

Figure 8.1   Business operating system priorities
(adapted from Arnold S. Judson, 'Productivity Strategy and Business Strategy: Two Sides of the Same Coin,' *Interfaces*, January–February 1984)

Reaching congruence across functions

In our experience with managers both in manufacturing and service companies, this is a painful exercise. Seldom do managers from different functions agree. The finance representative inevitably pushes for the 'idol,' productivity. The engineer argues a strong case for flexibility. The market shouts for customer satisfaction. As noted in chapter 5, each of these priorities may be present but one should be dominant. And more importantly, it should be recognized and supported by each function in the business system.

Managers identifying priorities 1 and 5 as being of major import-ance believe that productivity is the driving force regardless of the lip service they may pay to customer satisfaction or flexibility. High points for priorities 2 and 4 suggest customer satisfaction as the driving concern. Finally, managers who highly rate priorities 3 and 6 believe flexibility should be the driving force.

Individual responses are summarized and analyzed for con-vergence or divergence of views between the different functions (operating managers, finance, quality, etc.). The results are fed back to all key managers in order to stimulate discussion on the key priorities of the BOS and of each department.

Reaching congruence at different levels of management

We are always surprised by the results of this exercise when com-pleted by different levels *within the same function*. By using the techniques described above, priorities are compared at the vice-president, director, manager, and supervisor level. More often than not, senior management is baffled by the fact that their message is not getting through to their employees. Originally we set aside one hour with clients to review this data. More often than not, it involves several hours with a follow-up meeting to resolve priorities.

The following example illustrates how actions speak louder than words.

For many years the construction department in a power company had built nuclear plants. However, when the demand for new nuclear plants slackened, the construction department activities shifted to modifications and maintenance of existing plants, including fossil fuel and hydroelectric plants. In nuclear con-struction the driving force was essentially 'quality at any cost.' However, in the new environment, the vice-president sang a new tune, with more balance between quality, responsiveness, and cost.

Unfortunately, his message was not heard by the lower man-agement ranks. The construction department sustained a reputa-tion for 'gold-plating' every job. In one instance, a doorknob needed replacement. However, since the door was scratched in a few places, the door and frame were sand-blasted and painted first. Then the doorknob was replaced. When these lower-level managers were questioned about current priorities, 'quality' came out top with everything else inconclusively jumbled as a distant second. The 'nuclear mentality' of 'quality at any cost' remained the ingrained driving force among the work team, even though their mission and strategies had changed dramatically.

Until there is a clear and unified understanding of direction and priority, there is no point in going further. As the old saying goes, 'If you're not sure where you are going, any road will take you there.'

The good, the bad, and the ugly

All is probably not hopeless with your measurement system. Salvage your good measures and discard the bad ones. Using the diagnostic tools described in this section is an effective way to get managers thinking about how the entire collection of measures in their department works on a day-to-day basis.

At first glance these diagnostic tools appear to overlap. To some degree that may be true. However, we have found that a comprehensive review and analysis of the current system by those affected by the new measurement scheme is required to facilitate the change process. While the exercises we describe in this section are technically helpful in designing the new system, their primary benefit is to get management to understand that there is a *problem* and accept *ownership* for the resolution to the problem.

Probing for critical performance measures issues

At your next department staff meeting ask the following questions. They provide a quick way to dig in and focus on issues important to the performance measurement system.

- *Do measures foster an environment of continuous improvement?*
  Is the feedback on the process germane to what needs to be done? Are measures reported over time? Are they benchmarked to competitors' performance and/or realistic goals?
- *Are the department's performance indicators clearly linked to the strategic objectives of the business that the department supports?*

Do measures help to focus on strategic actions? Do they promote organizational learning?

- *In developing measures, have managers taken into account supplier–customer networks?*
Is performance measured where two functions touch? Are internal customers even recognized?
- *Is the performance of the entire business system more important than local department measures?*
How well is teamwork encouraged across functional silos or divisional barriers?
- *Does one system/report take into account quality, delivery, cycle time, and waste?*
Are measures integrated and reviewed simultaneously?
- *Are comments solicited from customer(s) when quality and delivery measures are proposed?*
If departments develop their own self-gratifying measures of departmental performance, do customers have the final say?
- *Does the system focus on reducing cycle time?*
Is time an important measure? Are critical path lead times monitored closely? Is there a conscientious effort to maintain a fast *pace* in your operations?
- *Does the system help to focus on the right priorities?*
Are BOS priorities clear? Does management make local department priorities explicit?
- *Is the system responsive to changes in customer expectations?*
Are customer expectations quickly translated into operational imperatives?
- *Are reports simple, relevant, consistent, and used as a catalyst for operational improvement?*
Do measures support decisions? Are they organized to provide the appropriate detail, when needed?

These questions are designed to give you a rough assessment of how well your system is functioning. The more questions that are answered 'no' or 'not sure,' the less likely the control system is to be motivating the 'right' actions. For example, in one manufacturing company, only 5 percent of its managers could answer 'yes' to more than six questions. Similarly, in another survey of 35 managers from different companies, only 9 percent could say yes to six or more questions, while 70 percent felt the measurement systems let them down in at least seven of the areas!

This exercise serves three main purposes.

1 It establishes a *common language and focus*.
2 It gets managers to *define the problem* and *own the solution*.
3 It scopes out the project: does the measurement system need a *tune-up or a new engine*.

Profiling existing measures

By now you know what your BOS priorities should be and how well your current performance measurement system is functioning. The next step is to profile the measures you report today and highlight issues related to their purpose (e.g. operational review, goal setting, budgets, compensation, etc.) frequency, and importance, etc.

Two analyses are important here. First, this task forces you to list all measures reported in your department. This may point to problems such as too many measures or too infrequent reporting of vital statistics. Second, it points out how measurements are used and describes their impact on operations and on the organization as a whole.

Once you have listed all your measures, review them with the department management team. Rank the measures in order of importance to your department's mission or charter and to the business strategy. A simple A, B, C rating is sufficient: A indicating very important, B somewhat important, and C that the measure is inappropriate. Compare the rankings of key department managers. This exercise promotes a good deal of debate when managers disagree on the importance of different measures, and begin to focus on specific problems in your reporting system.

Once you have completed this part of the exercise, allot the measure to the most appropriate category: quality, delivery, cycle time, or waste. This exercise tells you how comprehensive or relevant your performance measurement system is. For example, customer satisfaction may be the number one goal of your business strategy, yet your department may not have any appropriate measures of quality or delivery!

After you complete this profile, summarize the message it sends to the people in your department. Is this the message you want to be received? Are your people being motivated to do the right things?

A critique of current measures

The quickest way to critique your current measures is to categorize them in terms of their strategic importance to the business. Use the measurements listed in your 'profile' and match them up to the following categories.

1 *Performance indicators that track strategy implementation and achievement*   These are the measures directly relevant to the performance of the strategic plan. Keep them. For instance, a large regional bank's strategy identified major opportunities to utilize its mortgage servicing database to cross-sell the bank's other services, such as consumer lending. In effect the strategy called for the mortgage servicing department to provide information to a new internal customer, the consumer lending department. 'Quality' and 'delivery' measures had been established to insure the mortgage servicing department met the needs of the consumer lending department so that the bank as a whole could profit. These measures were especially effective and obviously would remain in place following the measurement review.

2 *Measures that accord with what is needed to achieve your strategies*   These measures may not be directly linked to a specific strategy, but they may be just as important to strategic success. 'On-time delivery' is a frequently used measure for monitoring a new product introduction strategy. This measure would also remain in place after the measurement system has been restructured. Measures in this category are important and should be given added visibility and attention in the new measurement system.

3 *Indicators that are out of alignment with your business strategies*   These measures may not be wrong, but they may not be the most effective indicators required to sustain the organization's focus on strategies. Some reworking of the measure itself and/or where and when it is reported may be required. For example, a problem occurs when the sales department is measured quarterly, rather than weekly. This may encourage sales to be booked all at once near the end of the quarter, rather than evenly distributed throughout the quarter. The resulting surge of work, on order processing through the operations which produce and deliver the work, may be highly wasteful.

Perhaps the best example of measures out of alignment is in the brokerage firm which professes in its strategy to be 'customer-driven.' However, it measures its branches and brokers solely on revenues. A more relevant measure of 'customer satisfaction' would be to track how much money was earned for the customer.

4 *Measures that are irrelevant to strategy*   Some measures seem to have a life

of their own. They exist because they were relevant at one time, are feasible, and/or they make someone look good. In many cases these measures must be made for some regulatory or bureaucratic reason, but are not needed for managing operations. Consideration should be given to their elimination as indicators of operating performance.

For instance, measuring purchasing agents on purchase price variance (the difference between real price paid during the year from the quoted price standard set at the beginning of each year) is useless in a JIT environment. While these variances are fed into the accounting system to balance the ledger, their use as an indicator of performance cultivates collaboration with vendors solely on price rather than quality and JIT deliveries.

5 *Measures that are counterproductive and likely to defeat or delay strategic achievement* In many cases the traditional long-standing measures, such as cost accounting variances and productivity measures, have become obsolete and are now counterproductive. For instance, measuring equipment utilization at a non-bottleneck operation encourages the use of excessive work-in-process inventory to ensure that the equipment is running. Eliminate these measures immediately!

6 *Hidden, culturally driven measures undermining world-class performance* Correcting these measures is a difficult task, but probably represents the greatest potential to improve productivity in your department, and more importantly, the business system. The nuclear construction department case described earlier is a good example of cultural influence. Likewise, in a manufacturing company, when stating a JIT strategy, the management berates a floor supervisor for allowing a machine to sit idle. Although the formal measure is gone, there is a strong cultural bond to the old measure which sustains its influence on day-to-day operations. These culturally hidden measures need to be brought to the surface and explicitly replaced in the new measurement system.

If many of your existing measurements end up in categories 4, 5, or 6, major redefining of the measurement system is required. Furthermore you must take a fresh look at what strategically important indicators are missing in the business system.

External measures

World-class performance begins by identifying the performance that counts to your customers (see chapter 6). Translating the needs of the customer starts with identifying your department's immediate internal and external customers from the workflow chart (see chapter 4 on mapping). If your department's customer is an external customer of the business, see marketing and sales or the quality group for information concerning customer expectations or review customer feedback, complaints, etc. Make sure your management team agrees on the identity of your department's customer(s) and, if more than one, which customers are most important.

Once the major *internal* customers are identified, talk to them about their expectations concerning your department as a supplier. The following questions may be helpful in determining their needs.

1 How does the customer define the quality of your department's output? What is the customer's definition of good quality (and bad quality)?
2 How does the customer define 'good' delivery of supplier's output?
3 What is the driving force or major concern of your customer? For example, is the customer more concerned about quality or flexibility?
4 How frequently does the customer need information on supplier's quality and delivery performance?
5 How can the channels of communication be improved?
6 What early warning signals are in place if quality or delivery falls below customer expectations?

This questionnaire should be used as a two-stage process. First, get your management team to predict how the customer will answer. This can be most easily accomplished in a group discussion at a department staff meeting. Then, have the manager of each major customer answer the same questions. Compare the responses and make an appointment with the manager of the customer department to discuss and resolve major differences. Finally, draft your quality and delivery measures (definition, methodology, frequency, etc.) and obtain customer acceptance.

Internal measures

As described in chapter 7, internal measures focus the operation on doing more with less time and money. Measured like golf, improvement is going the same distance with less effort (fewer swings, less walking off-course, and therefore less time).

Cycle time checklist

Define the extent to which the cycle time measures must be detailed. With two questions and a simple calculation, it is possible to discover a department's opportunity for improvement.

Department: _____   **Date:** _____

☐ **DURATION**: Note how many hours (days or weeks) it typically takes for a unit of work to go through the department, from the time it enters the department until the time it leaves

☐ "HANDS-ON" TIME: Note the hours (days or weeks) the unit is actually being worked on (by a person or machine). In other words, how long would it take to hand carry the work through the process with no delays?

☐ "HANDS-ON" TIME/DURATION: Calculate the percentage of the duration that the unit of work is actually being worked on

---

Figure 8.2   Cycle time checklist

Figure 8.2 provides a simple guide to evaluate the cycle time reduction opportunity.

- If under 10 percent, it is a major priority area for improvement; more specific subdepartment, and/or product-focused cycle time measures, are required.
- If between 10 and 30 percent, there is significant room for improvement; some focus and emphasis should be placed on the major portions of the cycle or specific products (units of work) which contribute to the low 'Hands-on' time percentage.
- From 30 to 50 percent is better than most cycles; it must be measured but not much detail is required.
- From 50 to 100 percent is much better than most cycles; it must be measured, but no additional detail is required.

Checklist for identifying waste

It is helpful to group non-value-added activities, whether direct or overhead, in appropriate waste buckets: inventory, equipment and facilities, processing operations, or rework. Although these sound like manufacturing terms, they are not. Paperwork on the purchasing agent's desk is work-in-process. An incorrect order configuration by the salesperson is waste.

We have regrouped some of Canon and Toyota's waste categories (previously illustrated in table 7.1 and exhibit 7.1), into a program that we have called – since America is so diet-conscious – 'Eliminate all FATS' (see exhibit 8.1).

Exhibit 8.1 Eliminate all FATS

*F*ailures	scrap
	rework
	warranty costs
	cost of corrective actions
*A*ppraisals	incoming inspection
	any checking activity
*T*asks	unrelated to the workflow
	used for expediting
*S*urplus	inventory over process time
	labor costs due to downtime
	unused equipment and space

Simply reporting waste is not the point of the exercise. Continuous improvement in everything means eliminating waste (the Japanese term for this is *kaizen*). The worksheet shown in figure 8.3 can be used to focus the attention of all employees on the task at hand. Identify and quantify the specific waste (columns 2 and 3). Your finance department should have most of this data readily available (overtime dollars, rework, scrap, incoming inspection costs, etc.). Then estimate the percentage by which you can reduce waste over a set time (column 4). This exercise can help in identifying and prioritizing improvement opportunities. Be sure to also make it clear who is responsible for the waste reduction effort (column 6) and get commitment to a schedule (column 7).

The following guidelines are useful when developing, reporting, and eliminating waste.

Category	Description of specific costs	Cost ($)	Improvement potential (%)	Improvement potential ($)	Responsibility	Schedule
F Failures						
A Appraisals						
T Tasks						
S Surplus						

Figure 8.3   FATS worksheet

1 It is management's responsibility to report all waste in their particular department.
2 Eliminating waste should be viewed as an opportunity to help the business's cost performance.
3 Everyone is accountable for managing their activities effectively (doing the right things) and efficiently (doing them well).
4 At no time can anyone compromise quality and delivery for cost (e.g. cut overtime but miss delivery).
5 The department that incurs the cost reports the waste. For example, the materials department should report inspection as waste, even though purchasing created the need (i.e. by purchasing an item that had to be inspected).
6 There should be no finger pointing. Manage expectations and performance with internal suppliers as you would with external vendors.

A word about indices

Managers may elect to combine several measurements into a composite index in order to give a more complete picture of performance. For example, at the department level, one may elect to report one 'waste rate' number which is made up of scrap, rework, excess work-in-process, etc. Waste could also be defined as the dollar value of in-process, rejected materials as a percentage of total input materials. Similarly, one may look to developing a 'quality rating' for a supplier. That index may include quality of design, percent on quality vendor list (QVL) process design, and mean time between failures (MTBF). A plant manager may want a single score for his plant's productivity, such as total factory productivity (outputs/inputs). This measure is a composite of business system performance taking into account delivery and cost. Exhibit 8.2 summarizes the major advantages and disadvantages of using indices.

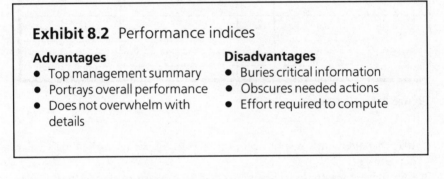

Exhibit 8.2 Performance indices

Advantages	**Disadvantages**
• Top management summary	• Buries critical information
• Portrays overall performance	• Obscures needed actions
• Does not overwhelm with details	• Effort required to compute

Exception reporting

While indices are helpful to convey a message, they must not bury or obscure the causal relationship behind the indices. The measurement system must enable the root causes of any major problem to be pinpointed. One way to accomplish this objective is to establish ceilings and floors for the components of the index and generate exception reporting when any individual measure exceeds the parameters.

If production waste rate includes work-in-process inventory, scrap, rework, incoming inspection, and overtime, the inventory number may overpower the other data. For example, inventory may be going down, showing improvement in the overall index even though overtime has been on the rise. When the overtime percentage exceeds an established parameter, the variable is highlighted to alert management to the problem.

In general, if any component of an index is so important, report it separately. For example, if rework and scrap are both issues, report both data.

Reporting guidelines

Design a simple, consistent format

In order for any measurement system to be effective, there needs to be a succinct and visually simple record card that all employees can understand. The scorecard should have at least four measures (one for each performance criterion) and probably fewer than ten (see figure 8.4).

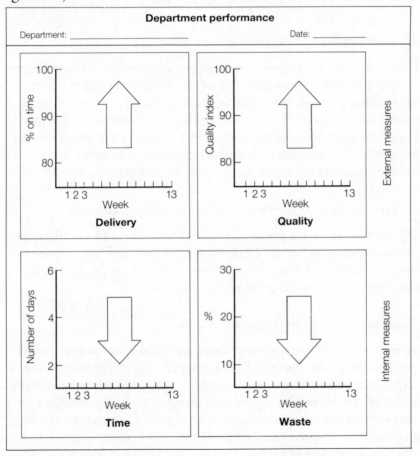

Figure 8.4 Performance report card

Show a balanced profile of performance

When reviewing the performance of your department, the four performance criteria should always be shown together to avoid mixed performance signals. In many companies that we have visited, quality is reported by quality control, cost by accounting, and output by distribution. With that kind of fragmented reporting, trade-offs are hard to identify, let alone understand.

Hold people accountable for what they can control

The process described in steps 6 and 7 of figure 9.1 establishes measures that managers can affect.

Measure and manage performance over time

Charts are useful in that they are not snapshots of performance frozen in time but rather show how the BOS and its component functions are moving through time. In this respect, the report card provides a profile of performance relative to previous performance. The intention is to encourage continuous improvement over past performance, as well as to reach performance goals and objectives. In cyclical businesses, it may be more appropriate to plot similar time periods.

Add control limits to account for random statistical fluctuation

Figure 8.4 can be transformed into a control chart by adding upper and lower control limits.[1] In this way managers will not overreact to chance variation in the process. Control charts can be used to focus corrective action when a real problem exists.

Focus on continuous improvement

A measurement system must foster an attitude of continuous improvement in all aspects of performance. Therefore, the feedback from the measurement system should be positive when improvement is made. For example, reporting that there was improvement in a delivery measure sends positive feedback and rewards throughout the business system even though 100 percent on-time delivery (the ultimate goal) was not met.

In the format illustrated in figure 8.4, quality and delivery measures are always defined in such a way that improvement is recorded as an increase in the measure (we got better). Conversely, continuous improvement in cycle time and waste is shown as a decrease in the measures (we are cutting out time and waste).

To get some idea whether the rate of improvement is good or bad, and what is a realistic objective, is not easy. However, one interesting approach developed at Analog Devices Inc. (ADI) is the estimation of rate of reduction, or how long a 50 percent improvement in a measure would take by type of problem.[2] Here 'type' refers to whether a problem is 'unifunctional,' 'cross-functional,' or 'cross-divisional.' ADI's research suggests that unifunctional problems can be cut in half in about 3 months, cross-functional ones in 9 months, and cross-divisional problems in 18 months. 'Defects' (e.g. late delivery, poor quality) are plotted on semi-log paper so that the half-life can be calculated from the slope of the line.

For example, to reduce late deliveries by 50 percent may take 9 months. If current deliveries are 10 percent late (or 90 percent on time) and the theoretical minimum is 2 percent late (i.e. due to credit problems, late customer pick-up, etc.) in one half-life, late delivery would be cut to 6 percent late (or 94 percent on time). If improvement activities are maintained, in another 9 months later deliveries would be reduced to 4 percent late. In other words, in 18 months, on-time delivery would improve from 90 to 96 percent (see figure 8.5). Figure 8.6a depicts the situation where continuous improvement may be enough to surpass and stay ahead of the competition. However, one must guard against complacency. It may be that a competitor will make a great surge in performance. That possibility should not be overlooked. Or, perhaps more importantly, could your

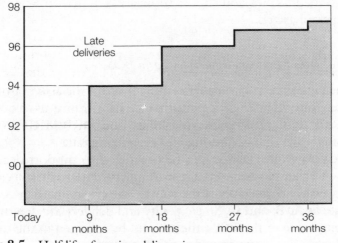

Figure 8.5   Half-life of on-time delivery improvements

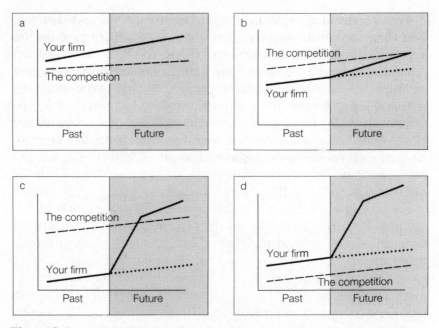

Figure 8.6 (a) Continuous improvement may be sufficient; (b) accelerated improvement is required; (c) breakthrough improvement is required; (d) breakthrough improvement is desired

firm make a great surge in performance and devastate the competition? That potential should be explored. The point is to understand your rate of improvement and its position relative to the competition, and then to pick and choose those areas of performance which must be emphasized.

Show relationship between department and BOS

Most managers we talk to never complain about the amount of data available. With gigabytes of performance data churning out of test equipment, numerical control machines, and DRP/MRP systems, the issue is really one of filtering and organizing data.

Here is how information can be organized to support decision-making. A business system report spanning three departments (A, B, and C) would be made up of the sum of the critical path cycle time and waste in A, B, and C. Since quality and delivery are determined by the customer of the BOS, they would be reflected in the quality and delivery measures of the department furthest downstream (C).

Each component of the BOS would report their waste and cycle time and their quality and delivery performance as defined by their customer, the immediate downstream department.

With this kind of reporting and interaction among departments, managers are not penalized for 'exceeding budget' if overall system costs are lowered. As a means of measuring success, this approach requires local management to focus on the next department's needs and the overall values set by the end-customer. Scorecards for both the department and the BOS should be highly visible to all employees.

When continuous improvement is not enough

Resting on one's laurels when a certain milestone is achieved, however, is a sure way to fall behind the competition. As Will Rogers once said, 'Even if you're on the right track, if you sit still, you'll get run over.' Also management must concern themselves with the *rate of improvement*. A 5 percent improvement may be good, but if the competition improves by 10 percent (assuming the same starting place), it is not good enough. The slope of the continuous improvement curve must be compared with that of your best competitor.

The magnitude of difference between current performance and required performance determines the extent to which improvement is emphasized and rewarded, or performance to goal is emphasized and rewarded.

Improvement can be emphasized when performance is close, equals, or exceeds that of your competitors. However, when a competitor's performance is significantly higher it may be necessary to emphasize performance to a goal which has been, in effect, established by the competition. Xerox calls this 'benchmarking.' They have gone far beyond simply comparing product between themselves and each competitor. It is the responsibility of each department to 'benchmark' their performance to that of the best in their industry. This benchmarking philosophy transcends the directly competitive departments, such as R&D and manufacturing, to encompass all departments, including finance and personnel.

Accelerated improvement

Figure 8.6b depicts two performance slopes. Assume that the lower line is your performance and the higher line reflects the competitor's performance. In this scenario, continuous improvement is not enough because the competitor is improving at the same rate. At any point in time, the difference in performance between you and the competitor remains the same.

The key is to first ascertain whether the attribute of performance is of strategic significance. Or are you competing for the same market but on differing aspects of performance? If the attribute of performance is important, it may be necessary to embark on a program of 'accelerated improvement.' Accelerated improvement means that your rate of improvement must be greater than that of your competitor in order to eventually surpass their performance.

Breakthrough improvement

Figure 8.6c demonstrates the case where a 'breakthrough improvement' is required just to catch up with the competition. In this situation, your company is so far behind that continuous improvement, or even accelerated improvement, will be insufficient. A breakthrough improvement in performance is required just to meet the competition.

However, why is your company not the one everyone else wants to catch up with? Figure 8.6d illustrates a breakthrough improvement in performance which puts your firm way ahead of the competition. A breakthrough of this magnitude is especially critical when a firm's strategy is to distinguish itself on a particular dimension of performance (e.g. Federal Express's 'positively overnight').

The only way to get a breakthrough improvement is to establish aggressive and wildly ambitious goals. For example, setting breakthrough goals such as cutting new product introduction time in half gets different functions working together for a common purpose and forces a fresh look at the business. Radical thinking replaces the conventional incremental improvement approach.

General Electric set a goal to reduce its order-to-finished goods time from 3 weeks to 3 days for its circuit breaker boxes. Starting from square one, GE management questioned everything about the way they were making the boxes. Breakthrough performance was achieved by consolidating six plants into one, reducing the number of parts by 95%, automating the factory and eliminating levels of management.[3]

Early warning systems

Tracy O'Rourke, CEO of Allen-Bradley, once said that 'Without the right information, you're just another person with an opinion.' One could also add that that information needs to be available at the time a decision is being made. Reporting frequency of critical information must also be tied to the time-span of decision-making. For example, a corporate vision may be set and/or assessed about every five years. Here long-term market share trends are important. Strategies are set every two to three years but need to be monitored more frequently (quarterly) to make sure actions are on track. BOS reports must be reviewed more frequently to provide feedback on critical operating systems. At the department level, feedback must be more frequent (weekly) for management to make decisions concerning scheduling, maintenance, staffing, etc. At the work-center level it must be very frequent – daily, or even more often where real-time data are available: for example, stopping the line if three bad parts are processed.

Managers at the business operating level, then, need only enough feedback to know when a problem exists that is going to affect total period performance. Small glitches are to be handled on the plant floor. Major problems should, on the other hand, be signaled as soon as possible. The reporting frequency at the lowest level of the performance pyramid provides exactly this type of response capability.

Exhibit 8.3 gives suggestions for structuring operations reviews in manufacturing above the plant floor level

---

Exhibit 8.3   Operating a performance review program

Executive committee

Scope	Content
Meets:	Quarterly
Includes:	CEO and function heads (e.g. R&D, marketing, manufacturing, distribution, etc.)
Purpose:	Review BOS scorecards (New product introduction, order fulfillment)
	Evaluate strategy execution
	Support resource decisions
	Identify cross-functional issues

Responsibilities:	Feedback to BOS management
	Exception reporting
	Commitment process

BOS review (Business operating system)

Scope	*Content*
Meets	Monthly
Includes:	Project leaders
	Major customers
Purpose:	Review BOS scorecards
	Evaluate programs
	Support resource decisions
	Explain peformance outliers
Responsibilities:	Feedback to local management
	Exception reporting
	Problem identification

Department reviews (components of a BOS)

Scope	*Content*
Meets:	Weekly
Includes:	Local management team
	Internal customers
Purpose:	Review local performance
	Interpret BOS priorities
	Evaluate activities
	Early warning signals
Responsibilities:	Feedback to local operations
	Exception reporting
	Problem resolution

Summary

In order to smash your old yardsticks and replace them with new measurement devices, you must:

- look before you leap: understand and effectively communicate the priorities critical to your business system
- break down the physical and emotional links with the old measurement systems
- build on the current measures that are doing the job
- throw out those measures that have no place in the new competitive environment

- rethink your quality and delivery measures if they do not reflect your customers' expectations
- forget about the way you used to think about productivity; productivity is not about cost reduction, but about profit maximization
- use a simple consistent format to present the few critical measures you need to manage your activities
- benchmark your performance to that of your best competitor. Do not settle for continuous improvement if quantum improvements are required.

This chapter presented the tools required to design new yardsticks in a simple supplier–customer relationship. This is a good place to start. However, the ultimate benefit of changing the yardsticks and the corporate culture itself, is found in large-scale implementation throughout the company. This will be the subject of the next chapter.

Notes

1 For a good explanation of control charts see: William S. Messina, *Statistical Quality Control for Manufacturing Managers* (John Wiley, New York, 1987).
2 Arthur S. Schneiderman, 'Setting Quality Goals,' *Quality Progress*, April 1988.
3 Brian Dumaine, 'How Managers Can Succeed through SPEED,' *Fortune*, February 13, 1989.

9

◇

Altering the Corporate Mindset

◆

What gets measured gets done. If you are looking for quick ways to change how an organization behaves, change the measurement system.

Mason Haire, University of California,
Institute of Industrial Relations

In chapter 2, we said that companies must change the corporate mindset concerning short-term financial scorecards, MBO, functional organizations, technology, and the traditional accounting model. Management must take a fresh look at activities and learn how to satisfy the needs of the customer, the stockholder, and employees simultaneously.

There really are no quick ways to change mindsets, but there are ways to get the process started and leapfrog over barriers to change.

Holding out the umbrella

The performance measurement system described in this book will not be easily implemented unless top management have embraced the concept of total quality management. Changing the yardsticks requires an umbrella over it to allow it to flourish. For those companies well on the way down the organizational learning curve, the performance measurement approach described here is a tool to help reinforce, motivate, and monitor continuous improvement. Companies that preach quality but do not organize for it will get shortchanged.

144

Only top management can make this change by leading in the quality improvement effort and involving all employees in the program.

Awareness

For years, management has been measuring a straight line with a yardstick. As noted in chapter 2, the system worked for a while in a seller's market. Today, managers are being asked to measure a circle using the same old yardstick. They are often faced with two choices:

1 To try to adapt the old tool to solve the new problem.
2 To measure only those things that the old tool was designed to measure.

Of course, there is a third alternative: use a new tool. Like any other tool, the user must be fully trained on the tool's uses and operating instructions.

All managers in the business operating system should attend an awareness training session on performance measurement. The objectives of the session are to explain:

- why traditional performance measures are counterproductive
- how, through effective measurement and control, strategic plans will result in strategic performance
- the specific linkages between top-level business measures and day-to-day operational measures
- why it is important to differentiate between internal and external measures and how to understand their relationships
- an effective means of managing the implementation of a system to measure and control strategic performance
- how to organize and structure reports which encourage corrective action.

Establishing cross-functional teams

The performance measurement system must be integrated across organizational boundaries as defined by the BOS. The team responsible for changing the yardsticks should include:

- the perceived leader in the BOS

- each manager in the supplier–customer network
- one individual within each BOS to act as the overall BOS measurement analyst.

Education and training

Those involved in designing the new yardsticks need to receive intensive training. This can be accomplished by internal training or the use of outside consultants. Upon completion of the training, the team will have had hands-on practice with the various worksheets described in chapter 8 and be able to:

- develop a common understanding of a company's business priorities
- identify measurement problems that could prevent a department from achieving strategic objectives
- structure the team effort required to define departmental indicators of success
- develop measures that count to the customer – and the bottom line
- format and present information for different levels of decision-making.

The implementation plan

Once management is committed to the need to revitalize their operational control system, attention is turned to implementation. A detailed plan such as the one outlined in figure 9.1 provides a useful road map.

Step 1

Top management may select a business system using one or more of the following criteria.

- The business system is critical.
- It is of strategic importance.
- There is a perceived performance problem.
- There has been a recent workflow change.

Management then must select the team to conduct the measurement analysis and reshape the yardsticks.

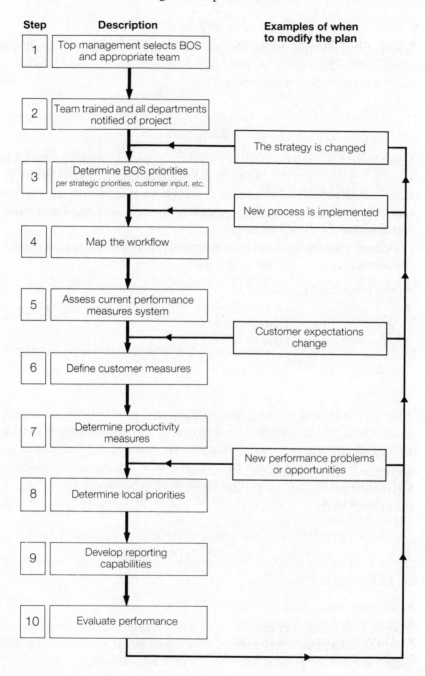

Figure 9.1   Implementation plan for changing the yardsticks

Step 2

Everybody on the team should be familiar with the concepts explained in chapters 4–8. They should have a working knowledge of the tools provided in chapter 8.

Step 3

Use figure 8.1 to determine key strategies and priorities in the BOS in which the program is being implemented. Department staff meetings constitute a useful forum in which to brainstorm on driving forces in the BOS. It would be useful to invite senior management to the first part of these meetings.

Follow up with a meeting to review the results. Make sure there is consensus on:

- the boundaries of the BOS
- the emphasis given to priorities (e.g. should more attention be given to customer satisfaction?)
- priorities across different functions.

Step 4

Map the workflow, as described in chapter 4, to identify your department's immediate suppliers and customers. Consult with operating management and/or your industrial engineering department as required. When identifying the department relationships within a component of a BOS, it is important not to get bogged down in detail. Remember that the primary intent is to recognize and identify the *major flow of work*.

Mapping is the key to identifying operations without value added (e.g. why is something moved twice, or inspected?).

Step 5

Assess your current control system using the techniques described in chapter 8. Interview key members of your operating team separately and compare the results. We suggest that you develop a simple index for responses to the questions on p. 125, such as that given in exhibit 9.1.

Exhibit 9.1   Diagnostic index

Response	Diagnosis
5 or more 'no' or 'not sure'	Your performance measurement system is out of tune and probably counterproductive
3 or 4 'no' or 'not sure'	Part of your performance measurement system needs to be replaced
1 or 2 'no' or 'not sure'	The system may only need fine-tuning

Profiling your existing measures as suggested in chapter 8, leads to appropriate analysis and action.

- If you have too many measures, which ones can be eliminated?
- Some measures may have been required long ago, but may no longer be important. Can you drop them?
- Are compensation and reward plans in line with strategic objectives. For example, if you are pursuing a JIT strategy, are you rewarding buyers on purchase price variance, which may add to lead times?

Finally, critique the system.

- Are hidden measures the real driving force (e.g. do not get caught without a spare)?
- Are some measures simply wrong? (Some people will need convincing.)
- What measures are missing?
- Why do you have masses of data and no information?

Step 6

Once you have identified the causal relationships in the workflow and critiqued the current measures, draft preliminary measures for your output. This exercise is most easily accomplished by holding a meeting with the key operating people in your function and completing a questionnaire similar to the one found in chapter 8. Then have your key customers answer the same questions. Analyze the differences.

Use this input to begin defining the measures.

Do not be discouraged by the number or magnitude of the gaps in your information network. If you know what you need but the data are not available, try defining a substitute measure or index. Even an educated guess about the right indicator is better than 100 percent accurate computer-generated information that is irrelevant to your strategy. Work to first simplify your information needs and then develop the appropriate delivery vehicle (on-line data, computer report, charts, phone call, etc.).

Go back to your (internal) customer to make sure both supplier and customer agree on the measures. If the customer has a complaint that your department is not directly responsible for (i.e. you passed along someone else's mistake), you need to know what problems exist and with what suppliers. This forces management to work together to sort out any difficulties. Figure 9.2 shows the detail behind incorrect and incomplete orders that supports the on-time delivery measure.

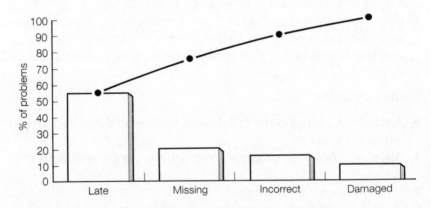

Figure 9.2   Customer order problems: (a) Pareto analysis; (b) corrective action focus

Step 7

Have your managers define their own internal goals for cost and process time using figures 8.2 and 8.3. This step will require a 1–2-hour meeting with key members of your department.

Step 8

Call a meeting with key operating people and review the measures developed. Ask the group to assess the challenge and agree on tactics to tackle the problem with the biggest benefits (opportunity for improvement). Discuss results and finalize priorities.

Step 9

In order for any measurement scheme to be effective, there needs to be a succinct and visually simple report card as depicted in figure 8.4. In that example, quality and delivery are always defined in such a way that improvement is recorded as an increase in the measure (arrow pointing upwards). Conversely, continuous improvement in cycle time and cost is recorded as a decrease in the measures (arrow pointing downwards). The four performance criteria should always be shown together when reviewing the performance of the BOS or one of its component departments. Trade-offs could also be addressed by emphasizing one criterion more than the others. Such charts are useful in that they are not snapshots of performance frozen in time but rather show how the operating system and functions are moving through time.

Reporting frequency should be on a need-to-know basis. At a work-center level, reporting should be frequent (e.g. on-line quality data) but it may only be necessary to report to senior management on a weekly/monthly basis at the BOS level.

Remember, at the department level, cost is measured in terms of waste. However, you need to keep track of total department costs since they are reflected in the BOS report. In this scheme for top-level reporting, the cost and cycle time measurements would be the sum of those for all departments. With this kind of reporting and interaction among departments, managers are not penalized for 'exceeding budget' if overall system costs are lowered.

Quality and delivery measures, on the other hand, are determined by the end-customer and therefore are reflected in the last department's external measures when reported at the BOS review. As a means of measuring success, this approach requires local management to focus on the next department's needs and the overall values set by the end-customer.

Do not be discouraged if it takes you months to put together a complete report. Typically there will be holes in the report: data not available, methodology not agreed to, supplier is uncooperative, etc. But do not lessen your expectations. Start with what you have identified as being critical to improving your performance.

The list given in exhibit 9.2, synopsized from chapter 8, can help in determining the fitness of your scorecard.

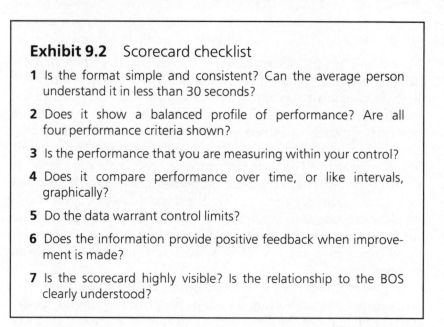

Exhibit 9.2   Scorecard checklist

1 Is the format simple and consistent? Can the average person understand it in less than 30 seconds?

2 Does it show a balanced profile of performance? Are all four performance criteria shown?

3 Is the performance that you are measuring within your control?

4 Does it compare performance over time, or like intervals, graphically?

5 Do the data warrant control limits?

6 Does the information provide positive feedback when improvement is made?

7 Is the scorecard highly visible? Is the relationship to the BOS clearly understood?

Step 10

Evaluate performance and seek continuous improvement in all four criteria. It is also important to make sure that measures are reported by the right people. For example, measures concerning the quality and delivery performance of your supplier must be reported by the supplier department. They must feel ownership – after all, they are responsible for the output and can affect it.

The bottom line in reporting, whether automated or manual, is to communicate essential information to the correct parties at the right time.

The implementation plan offers a practical structure for conducting the questionnaires and analysis described in chapter 8. There are two major milestones: the pilot program and the full implementation in the BOS.

Piloting the program

One of the features of the approach described in chapter 8 is that senior management can implement it in a modular fashion. It is not essential that the entire company switches over to using the BOS all at once. As a matter of fact, it is better to initiate the program on a small scale and demonstrate by example its tangible benefits. The program will have a domino effect. As each new department is pulled in by its customer, that department, in turn, must push the program upstream to its supplier, and so on, back to the beginning of the product or service creation process.

The pilot should involve a simple supplier–customer network. It is not essential, but is preferable, for the department to be near or at the end of the BOS. Since the external measures flow upstream, expansion is enhanced by having a solid grasp of the quality and delivery needs at the end of a BOS, usually the marketplace customer.

When to declare victory

The initial pilot effort should demonstrate how the approach works. During the first three months any publicity and visibility should be kept relatively low to allow the participants time to make it work.

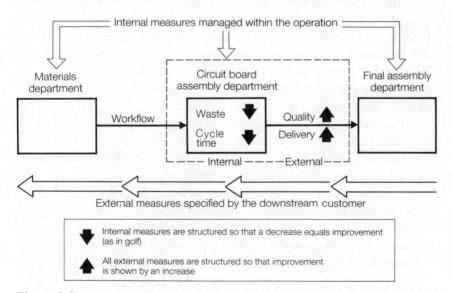

Figure 9.3 A pilot performance measurement system

Figure 9.3 illustrates how the new performance measurement system was piloted in a circuit board assembly operation. Quality and delivery performance measures were first developed for the department's output from the perspective of the customer (the final assembly department). Internal process time and cost goals were then established to best meet their external challenge. Next, the board assembly department worked out new quality and delivery measures with their suppliers (the materials department and the warehouse). In this way, new requirements and changing priorities were communicated as quality and delivery expectations from the downstream department.

Managers at the plant noted short-term side benefits from the new approach. Even before data were collected and reported, service improved from one department to the next because of the clearer focus and improved real-time dialogue between customer and supplier. In one instance, the circuit board assembly department believed that all the circuit boards they were sending to final assembly were operating satisfactorily. However, final assembly was saying that a large percentage of circuit boards were 'dead on arrival.' It turned out that the problem had existed for some time but the interactive effort demanded by supplier–customer analysis forced the issue to be addressed. The circuit board assembly department investigated and discovered that final assembly's means of measurement was inappropriate. They were uncovering defective cables as well as defective boards, but could not distinguish between the two. Working with the customer, the final assembly department, a new procedure was developed to properly segregate circuit board defects.

The new approach was a catalyst for improvement even before the first measures were recorded and reported.

After three months of implementation, management had eliminated 50 percent of the old measures. Virtually all the traditional cost variance measurements for internal process feedback were discarded, as well as any measures not agreed to by the customer.

One measure in particular was particularly troublesome to eliminate. In the traditional, pre-JIT, batch work order manufacturing environment, the materials department had established what appeared to be a reasonable measure of their performance called 'kit fill rate.' It measured the percentage of line items available, out of a belief that success meant having 98 percent of the required parts available for production. In the pre-JIT environment, where it took weeks to assemble a batch of circuit boards, the missing parts would arrive and be inserted before the boards were through the process anyway. The measure, as designed by and for themselves (the materials department), was used to measure the performance of the individual planners and the department as a whole.

Unfortunately, kit fill rate was irrelevant in the new manufacturing environment. When circuit boards could be assembled in a matter of hours, it made no sense to start the assembly until all the components were available to complete the circuit board. Therefore, if 2 percent of the parts were missing nothing could be built. The materials department could show an improvement in their kit fill rate with no actual improvement in production throughput. This measure was irrelevant to both the delivery and the quality dimensions of performance as defined by the customer of the materials department. Therefore, a new emphasis and measures were established with the materials department and the warehouse concerning timely delivery and the quality (completeness) of materials to circuit board assembly.

In addition to measures being eliminated, a significant number of them needed alteration, refinement, or redefinition. For example, cost was now defined in terms of waste: inventory, rework, scrap, overtime, and absenteeism. This meant that 'first pass yield' on the test equipment was no longer considered an indicator of quality. Since the rejects were repaired before sending the circuit boards to the final assembly department, the test and repair effort was now considered waste cost − the cost of getting it right prior to sending it to the downstream customer. The problem only becomes one of quality if it is detected by the customer.

Finally, some new measures had to be developed. For instance, the plant manager was pushing flexibility as the driving force in the plant, yet there were few tangible cycle time measures at the local operations level.

All over but the shouting

After the pilot period, management should expand upstream/downstream in the BOS and or begin pilots in other systems. The pilot team can play a coaching role to the new departments in the network. Sometimes converts make the best salespeople. The following comments are from managers who piloted the program:

- 'improves communication'
- 'makes you ask the right questions'
- 'highlights the irrelevancy of some current measures'
- 'problems become more visible'
- 'helps to fine-tune the whole operation'
- 'even though we have not finalized our reporting format, the quality from our major supplier has improved – because they better understood our expectations . . . and we would be monitoring their quality and delivery performance!'

Swimming upstream

Once the pilot program has been successfully completed, senior management can elect either to expand the performance measurement analysis gradually, taking in the next department, or to implement the entire BOS. We recommend the latter approach for several reasons:

- Clear priorities can be established for the entire BOS.
- The program can be implemented more consistently.
- There will be fewer disruptions.
- A complete team can be established.

When expanding the program, it is important to begin in the department furthest downstream if the pilot did not begin there. In this way, as the program moves upstream all departments are focusing on the end-customer.

Tips to overcome resistance

Hundreds of managers across a wide spectrum of industries have told us of their frustration with their company's resistance to changing the yardsticks. A group of managers at a conference on performance measures had no trouble listing causes of resistance:

- 'poor understanding of why new measures are needed'
- 'fear of failure'
- 'fear of the unknown'
- 'cost and time constraints'
- 'some people simply don't want to be measured'

- 'lack of patience by management, who favor the "instant pudding" approach'
- 'short-term perspectives'
- 'lack of trust and poor cross-functional teamwork.'

To overcome these obstacles, management can:

- clearly articulate the need for and importance of the project
- give appropriate support, time and resources
- hand-pick participants for the pilot
- use converted skeptics from the pilot to promote the program
- empower the people in the business to design the measures so that they feel ownership.

Other obstacles

Even when the program goes smoothly and the yardsticks are changed, other obstacles stand in the way of success. For example, the accounting system may send conflicting signals, people may be compensated on another set of criteria, there may be gaps in the information network, or work design and organization structure may prevent a clear focus on the BOS. These issues raise serious threats to new yardsticks and are discussed in some detail in the next chapter.

Summary

Expert tailoring often requires radical alterations. About the quickest way we can think of to alter the corporate mindset concerning performance is to change the measurement system. In this chapter, we have suggested a tried and proven methodology for implementing the concepts espoused in this book. Here are some useful tips.

- Make sure top management understands the program and will support the team.
- Tie the program to your company's quality or productivity improvement program. (If you do not have one of these, start one quickly!)
- Make sure that each team member is committed to the project and will continue to support the new measurement system by using the information for continuous improvement.

- Pick the business system where there is a perceived measurement problem.
- Pilot the concepts in several different business systems.
- Turn the program over to the operating managers for ongoing maintenance and updates.

10

◇

Mending and Remodeling
Related Systems

♦

It is thrifty to prepare today for the wants of tomorrow.

Aesop, 'The Ant and the Grasshopper'

Throughout this book we have argued that the new yardsticks for performance measurement must be customer-focused, flexible, and dynamic. As strategies and customer expectations change, so must the yardsticks. In fact, the yardsticks of tomorrow will bear little resemblance to those of the past: each measurement system will be tailored to the needs of the customer. As such, they will continually motivate operations against future requirements of the business.

The new yardsticks can be major tools to reinforce competitive behavior. They can also be used in reshaping, mending, and remodeling related systems: accounting, return on investment formulas, information systems, organization design, human resources, and compensation.

Mending the accounting system

New management initiatives, such as JIT manufacturing and total quality control, have exposed the informational and motivational shortcomings of traditional accounting systems. Feedback has been

The first section of this chapter, 'Mending the accounting system,' is adapted from C.J. McNair, K.F. Cross, and R.L. Lynch, 'Do Financial and Non-Financial Performance Measures Have to Agree?' *Management Accounting*, November 1990.

too aggregated, too late, too one-dimensional, or too irrelevant to be useful to operating managers. But the answer is not to scrap the accounting system.

Companies that create total performance measurement systems (that address customer satisfaction, flexibility, and productivity) should link such systems to the accounting system. Why? If top-level financial reports are built upon the accounting data, they need to be better synchronized with the operating measures. Otherwise, top management must rely on faith that the financial feedback will eventually move in the same direction as the operating performance measures. Furthermore, most senior managers we know will not take this leap. They continue to watch both scorecards. After all, they are held accountable for both! The trick will be to accomplish this linkage without affecting the integrity of the external financial reporting system or adding undue complexity to it.

Providing the right information at the right time

Control systems direct behavior, evaluate performance against preset goals, and provide information for adjusting the goals themselves through the feedback process. In current manufacturing accounting-based performance measurement systems, this loop is not complete. Variances, rather than serving to update goals (i.e. standards) are merely bled off to the general ledger. The underlying assumption, of course, is that the standards are right and reality is wrong. This assumption is at odds, for example, with the goals of JIT manufacturing.

Figure 10.1 illustrates a series of performance loops embedded in the performance pyramid introduced in chapter 5. Essentially, the base of the pyramid is a plan–do–check–act cycle (loop 1). Whether for an individual operation or the whole department, *non-financial measures*, such as on-time delivery, quality, cycle time, and waste, provide a complete control loop. Focusing in on the work center or department level, targets are set (e.g. reduction of waste or cycle time, improvement in quality), action takes place, and results are charted. Process adjustments are made, based on the results, to keep the system on track. These measures are timely, and close to the point of action. That means that feedback can be used to accurately adjust current activities. This is the definition of a complete control loop.

The business operating system level (see loop 2) actually consists

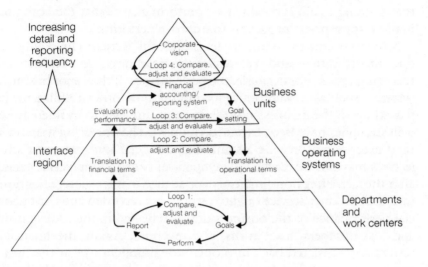

Figure 10.1 Performance loops

of a double set of controls: operating and financial. The former is used to evaluate how departments work together in meeting business system objectives. Financial reporting completes the control loop used at this level, translating the operating data into summary data for top management. For example, as improvements in cycle time are made at the department level, this information is passed up to the business system in the second performance loop (e.g. overall cycle time for the BOS). Adjustments are made to inventory to satisfy external financial reporting needs and the information is fed back into the goal-setting process in loop 1 (i.e. the goals are set more aggressively). Another example of how operating data is linked to the accounting system can be seen in how costs are handled. At the department level, non-value-added costs or waste are captured. At the plant level, total expenses from the general ledger are compared to the output. If total factor productivity goals (output/input) are not achieved, feedback and cost reduction activities are targeted at the departments reporting significant waste.

The feedback in loop 2 is not as timely as in loop 1. The time-span of decision-making at this level is longer. Most organizations are evaluated on monthly, or quarterly, performance. Managers at the BOS level need only enough feedback to know when a problem exists that is going to affect total period performance so that they can put in place appropriate programs to improve performance.

Moving up the pyramid, the level of detail decreases markedly, as does the definition, and realities, of the timeliness and frequency of reporting cycles. For example, the performance of the major business systems, such as new product introduction or order fulfillment, is passed up to the business unit/division/group level to evaluate how well strategies have been executed (loop 3). The operating measures (and exceptions) provide a signal that financial and marketing objectives may not be reached. The financial control loop verifies this, after the fact. Here non-financial data, such as market share, retention rate, and product/service quality ratings, are recorded and the financial performance of the business unit is reflected in the unit's profit and loss numbers, asset turns, and revenues. Again, the financial results are translated back into operational imperatives at the business system level. For example, if asset turn objectives for the business unit were not met, new programs are developed or emphasis is added to the cycle time measures in the business system to help improve financial performance.

The final feedback loop (loop 4) provides feedback on the corporate vision itself. Top management receives information over time on how effectively strategies have been executed and resources deployed. Total corporate performance is compared to expectations. Markets and competitive tactics are evaluated and adjusted as necessary.

In summary, the performance pyramid can support whatever type of reporting upper management wants. The detail is there, ready to be passed up through the reporting hierarchy on demand. Each level has its own tightly defined control loop as well as the means to access information from lower levels through the integrated system.

Switching from scorekeeper to coach

There needs to be some connection between the day-to-day operating signals and the accounting database when top management relies on summary financial measures from the accounting system. Up front, in the goal-setting process, financial goals need to be translated into operating terms. This requires strategic cost information. After the fact, the general ledger needs to be brought into line with operating realities. This is the world of cost control. Each of these requires a different view and a change in emphasis from 'relevance' to 'balance.'

'Strategic cost information' has one overriding objective: to provide relevant, timely information to support decision-making. It builds on prior results, serving as a database of trended results. The translation of financial accounting data into good management data is the world of activity accounting. This term captures the essence of the tie between costs and the activities that cause those costs. For each activity, a number of causal factors (e.g. drivers) can be identified. These drivers are the cause of downstream costs. They are also the basis for developing the productivity measures. By understanding activity costs managers can: focus improvement efforts on specific problems; make better business decisions regarding make-versus-buy and pricing; and, more importantly, prevent waste from occurring in the first place by analyzing 'bills of activity' for new products *before* costs are committed in volume production.

Focus on what counts the most

Three types of waste costs can be identified: detection, internal failure, and external failure. The existing general ledger structure of most companies can support this analysis on each of these dimensions. In terms of detection, account codes for quality control employees, incoming inspection equipment, supplies, etc., can be grouped together. Divided by the number of units produced in the same period, it provides a benchmark of the cost of detection. The operating system is given goals that reduce the underlying activities that generated the costs, based on the analysis of historical trends. The loop is closed by booking the production variances.

In this setting, as with activity-based costing, accounting adds value by focusing management attention on what needs to be done. Accounting-based precision and balance are not important. For practical reasons the calculations will consist of approximations and assumptions, but, the output will be relevant to the decisions at hand. The accountant's primary task is to re-pool existing account structures to match a new set of cost objectives

It is also important to remember that this information does not have to be recreated every day. In fact, it is only important when plans are being made, or the operating system signals that existing cost estimates are out of line.

Know when to play second fiddle

Another challenge for today's accountant is how best to maintain the equity of debits and credits without unduly distorting the reporting system. Some say that it is best to ignore it. But if top-level reports are built upon accounting data, the treatment of the balancing issue is critical to ensuring that top management gets consistent signals about performance in the plant. If balance is constantly forced in, though, distortions may occur whenever actual results do not match estimates – as is the case with volume variances. As any practicing manager knows, this is more the rule than the exception.

Two types of problems can occur in matching estimates to actuals: output variances and cost shifts. Output variance means that the actual mix or volume of sales may not match expectations. This can happen as a result of changes in the market, errors in forecasts, or process problems. By year end, though, most of these problems work their way out of the system. Output variances are, in a gobal sense, *compensating* (i.e. offsetting). A compensating variance is a 'mean regressing' phenomenon – over the operating period the estimate and the actual performance should be closely aligned.

In contrast, cost shifts cannot be controlled, nor is there any reason to believe they will reverse. Cost shifts, then, are *non-compensating* variances (i.e. they are not expected to wash out). In the non-compensating case, the mean has shifted. For example, products will always cost more if material or labor prices rise. Similarly, if quality improvement efforts result in permanent yield enhancements, then standards need to be updated.

Having separated these two events, the appropriate accounting treatment emerges. For the non-compensating variances, the traditional accounting approach of writing the costs off to the appropriate inventory and expense accounts, on a monthly basis, makes sense. Is there a need to signal the variance back to top management? Yes. Should it be done through accounting reports or through operating reports? It would seem that operating managers will know about it before accounting does. The accountant, though, is the one charged with maintaining the integrity of the standards used to give credit to production for good units completed. The data, then, should be used to adjust the cost standards more frequently. The feedback loop on non-compensating variances is short.

What about compensating or offsetting variances? If these are passed immediately through to the ledger, and up to management, attention is focused on the past. The company may break the budget forecast into monthly segments, but reality has it that seldom will orders arrive in the same mix, volume, and period as the plan suggested. This simple fact of life is the source of immense friction between production and marketing.

The accounting treatment of the compensating variances is straightforward. Just as 'buffers,' or contra accounts, are used to store reserves for bad debts and related events, why not set up an inventory contra account to hold output variances? Since what is important is the final performance for the year, monthly reconciliation just does not make sense. According to generally accepted accounting principles and the 1986 Tax Recovery Act, these costs must eventually be put into inventory, but the requirements of the law can be handled through an end-of-period adjustment.

The accounting variance does not add information to the analysis – it takes it away. Forcing balances to compensating variance accounts is non-value-adding activity of the worst kind because it trickles through the organization, promoting improper decisions and discord between functional units. Should compensating variances be fed back immediately into the standard cost system? No. Should they be used to provide strategic cost information in the next planning period? Definitely. Their value lies in letting management know what effect volume and mix variances have on annual performance.

Most progress is made through evolution, not revolution. There is no need to throw away the heart of the accounting system to make it more responsive to modern information needs. Nor is there any need to hang the management accountant in effigy. Instead, the accountant needs to be placed directly on the management team. He or she needs to take a pro-active role that puts the underlying demands of the general ledger system in its proper perspective. For too long the cart has been leading the horse. Balancing journal entries occurs after the fact; it does not help management make better decisions. It simply means that the underlying reporting system has integrity – important at year end to auditors, not daily to operating managers.

Remodeling the return-on-investment model

Customer satisfaction and flexibility are now critical dimensions of corporate success formulas. Technology, often viewed as a productivity weapon, can have a powerful impact on these newer competitive elements. Computer-integrated manufacturing technologies enable companies to offer more product variety and to customize products to order. Product technologies such as custom chips give customers more functionality in smaller boxes. Custom chips also change the nature of printed circuit board production – requiring less board-stuffing activities. Technology also changes the speed of work across organizations. For example, CAD/CAM is enabling companies to introduce products twice as fast. Imaging technology is enabling white-collar workers to respond to customers in record time.

In chapter 2, we presented some of the follies of believing that technology alone can save the day. Successful companies in the 1990s will be the ones that make the best investments in new technologies. Therefore managers must learn to measure technology's promise and reap the full benefits. Return-on-investment formulas must extend far beyond the simple labor savings in department X calculations and measure the impact on quality, service, responsiveness, and waste reduction across the entire business system.

Harnessing technology in a BOS

Managers who fully appreciate the role of technology in business systems and apply the correct technology can gain competitive advantage. There are four advantages that must be harnessed and focused on the needs of the customer.

Speed

Technology-related investments can certainly speed up processing. Using computerized credit checks, a mortgage company can now approve mortage applications in 15 minutes. By automating a factory that builds circuit breakers, an electronics company has cut the time from order to finished goods from three weeks to three days. These examples of responsiveness pay huge dividends in terms of market share gain and higher productivity. However, unless operations are first simplified and then integrated as a business system – that is, a set of integrated activities – automation may only help you do the wrong things faster.

The speed of changeovers embedded in factory automation

technology also provides manufacturers with the ability to increase the variety of product mix. For example, companies that have integrated robots, numerical control machines, and automated material handling systems can respond to increasing customer demands much faster. The ability to routinely and rapidly customize product to customer order provides a new source of competitive advantage. However, many managers must change their mindsets from being volume-oriented to being responsive to mix. Changing performance measures from a cost savings to a flexibility focus is one way to help foster this evolution.

Capability

Technology can provide the capability to consistently perform tasks and to consistently manage processes. In factories, robots spray-paint cars in the same consistent manner car after car. In offices and service businesses, computers and electronic mail provide the capability for the CEO, or anyone, to rapidly deliver the same consistent message to all levels of the organization. Technology enables financial service firms to manage multiple transactions and financial service offerings without error or delay. These technological capabilities allow for new levels of competitive performance, especially as related to consistent high levels of product and service quality.

Activity

Technology – whether product- or process-related – is reshaping the nature of work itself. For example, as chip manufacturers put more and more functionality on custom chips, computer manufacterers need fewer printed circuit boards to accomplish the same functionality. Also, by eliminating the need to link hundreds of chips into a system, custom chips both reduce manufacturing costs and improve reliability by eliminating the possiblity of faulty connections. As mentioned above, companies need to update their cost accounting systems to capture the true productivity gains masked by declines in inventory levels and direct labor. Bob Kaplan points out that under traditional cost accounting systems, decreases in direct labor and inventory levels cause 'unfavorable variances' because the actual costs absorbed into inventory are less than the applied overhead. This accounting entry sends the wrong signal (unfavorable) to operations and ignores the more germane question of whether the right overhead activities are in place to support the workflow. Also, as the rate of technology innovation speeds up, the focus of cost management shifts from production activities to the upstream product planning and development activities.

Information

Computers are ubiquitous in companies. They are found in formal planning and control systems, as well as in CAD/CAM systems and in microprocessors that are embodied in or attached to manufacturing equipment. New technologies such as bar coding, robotics, and programmable controllers have the capacity to churn out tremendous volumes of data in real time. Managers must learn how to filter these data to capture meaningful process information.

Managing technology for competitive effectiveness

Leading edge companies are building an arsenal of competitive weapons to win in the marketplace on the basis of customer satisfaction and flexibility. But to ensure success companies need to do more than clarify strategies and identify new technologies. They must convince top management to make the investment and reset the stockholders' expectations for immediate (quarterly) results.

Caterpillar's bold automation strategy is a case in point.[1] The company is investing $1.8 billion in plant modernization over a six-year period. Caterpillar's Chairman, George A. Schaefer, admits the company has taken a risky long-term gamble. But what choice is there when their competition, in particular, Japanese manufacturer Komatsu Ltd, already has built a network of hi-tech plants? From Caterpillar's perspective the investment is a matter of survival, yet Wall Street expressed concern in 1989 when earnings were flat. The investment is expected to save $1.5 billion a year when the program is completed in 1992. To justify its plant modernization program ('Plant with a Future') operating managers and accountants overhauled their return-on-investment model. The new model captures benefits from improved material flow, increased flexibility, improved quality, reduced inventory, indirect labor support costs, and manufacturability. The Caterpillar model also captures these benefits across the entire business system. Caterpillar evaluates investments in what they call 'bundles.' A bundle is a homogeneous segment of work or product that has common elements relative to processing and support systems (common elements include size of component, type of component, process, or location). The bundling technique ensures that the full impact of related costs and benefits is captured, the investment is evaluated in the context of the entire business system (plant), duplication of benefits is avoided and benefits are trackable after implementation.

The same case for automation applies to service companies as well. For example, Chris Routleff-Jones of the Western Provident Association in the UK, claims that investments in new technology such as imaging provides a competitive advantage in the health insurance market because 'it brings down the time it takes to process claims . . . and that means happy customers.'

Still, top management and investors will need convincing. Labor savings in a department are easy to compute and understand. Unfortunately, as noted in chapter 2, the savings made are often mythical. To capture real new benefits, companies must measure the impact of new investment on the criteria of improved quality and delivery, and reduced cycle time and waste. The goal of a performance measurement system is not only to help companies to conform to evolving technologies and strategies, but to nurture this learning. It should help companies adapt new technologies for competitive advantage – faster.

Custom tailoring executive support systems

With the advent of powerful desktop computers that can be connected to mainframe databases, a logical extension of 'measuring what is important' is automating the information environment for improved planning and control purposes.

Since the first computers began churning and spitting out data, managers have been trying to harness that power to make more informed decisions. Computers begat management information systems (MIS) departments – full of programmers, operators, and systems specialists who did mysterious things behind glass walls. MIS begat user groups, who had specific information demands. User groups begat decision support systems (DSS), allowing analysts to query databases, analyze the information, and simulate the impact of their decisions. DSS begat executive information systems (EIS) once executives became comfortable with the idea of a personal computer on their desk. Finally, EIS begat executive support systems (ESS), giving top executives windows to the bottom floors of the organization.[2]

But in a flatter, more responsive organization, it is not just the CEO who needs feedback on how things are going and what needs fixing. An information system should be able to provide any decision-makers, regardless of title, the right information at the right time. David Friend, chairman and president of Pilot Executive Software, a leading EIS vendor based in Boston, recognizes the significance of matching information to user need. In a play on the acronym EIS, Friend is calling EIS 'everybody's' information system. For example, a group manager could look at the group's financial performance. If strategic objectives were not being met, the manager could focus on the division level to see which plant's performance might need attention. With another click of the mouse, graphs of cycle time and waste appear. The manager can then call up the details of the waste: rework, scrap, inspection costs, excess inventory, overtime, etc. A department manager can then explain:

We had trouble with a key piece of equipment. It had not been properly maintained, which explains the increase in rework and in-process scrap. We have already developed a preventive maintenance schedule to prevent future surprises. We had to work the overtime to make up for unplanned downtime while our engineer performed the necessary maintenance.

If the purpose of performance measures is to motivate behavior leading to continuous improvement in customer satisfaction, flexibility, and productivity, all knowledge workers need access to key information. As noted earlier, the frequency and detail required is dependent on the type of decision at hand. If executives start checking up on local operations, the tendency could be for them to start making day-to-day, transaction-oriented decisions instead of more critical, longer-term strategic decisions.

Several software houses, including Pilot (based in Boston, Massachusetts) and Comshare (based in Ann Arbor, Michigan) have designed powerful EIS tools. In fact, Apple's 'Hypercard' and Wang's 'Freestyle' give users the capability to design 'stacks' of information in stand-alone systems, although they have size and data updating limitations. While EIS technology is available today, a word of caution is necessary. Just as companies learned the hard way about factory automation, they must be aware that software alone is not the solution. Getting the wrong kinds of data more quickly will not make anything better. You must first determine what is important, simplify your information requirements, and think through who needs what information and when.

If EIS is installed merely as a tool to change the look and feel (i.e. screens and graphics) of existing financial and sales data or to increase the frequency of reporting, companies are missing the real potential of this nascent technology. For example, senior executives may not need more frequent information. Overreacting to short-term fluctuations may lead to poorer decisions.

The real benefit of EIS lies elsewhere. EIS gives companies more than just the opportunity to define their information system priorities. It allows them to:

- push down decision-making by giving workers the information they need to respond to opportunities more quickly
- filter through huge amounts of data to tailor reports for different users
- share information easily between workers (regardless of function) in the same workflow
- improve organizational lending
- use internal performance measurement data as a sales tool.

Analog Devices' use of Pilot's EIS is a good example of how EIS can be used as a catalyst for improvement.[3] Analog has customized its EIS to provide a corporate scorecard (financial and non-financial data), customer services metrics (quality and delivery), manufacturing metrics (cycle time and yields), and a complete product-tracking system. The non-financial metrics are graphed over time, with upper and lower control limits and half-life goals. Reviewing this kind of information lets top management know whether strategic objectives are on track and whether performance deviations are normal fluctuations or need immediate attention. Employees at Analog know what top management considers important and can readily identify with corporate goals. For example, users (not restricted to executives) can look at overall on-time delivery performance, then drill down for the area of responsibility (e.g. whether it is a warehouse, factory, or credit problem) and pinpoint areas for improvement efforts.

Art Schneiderman, Analog's vice-president for quality and productivity improvement, uses quality and delivery information on key accounts when he meets with customers. By showing customers that Analog is concerned with what is important to them, EIS becomes a strategic marketing tool!

New styles for organizations

The new yardsticks foster learning throughout the entire organization by continually relating actions and measures to strategic objectives. When this happens a major change occurs in the corporate culture. Focus shifts from 'managing by the numbers' at the top, to continuous improvement in activities at business system level that provide competitive advantage. Thinking in terms of the business system emphasizes the need to work across functional boundaries. With a horizontal perspective on the workflows that deliver value to the customer, managers and employees are encouraged to think and act more as a team, both with respect to functions and with respect to issues of balancing customer satisfaction, flexibility, and productivity. As this perspective takes hold, it supplants the underlying logic of viewing organizations as a collection of separate functions.

The cross-functional team does not necessarily mean a revolution in structure, only changes in skills and style – particularly of leadership. The BOS orientation implies that the leader of each team facilitates problem-solving and decision-making within the group. These activities require frequent feedback and score-keeping by each team.[4]

'Back to the future' – the cross-functional organization

Tom Peters maintains that decentralization was the right strategy when DuPont created the first modern divisionalized organization – that is, each small division contained all the functions, such as R&D, engineering, purchasing, manufacturing, distribution, and sales. In *Thriving on Chaos*, Peters maintains that decentralization is still the correct strategy. He advocates that companies return to that earlier, leaner, cross-functional form.[5] Peters gives managers three useful prescriptions that can make their organization more responsive:

1 Decentralize. When your division gets too big, decentralize again. Never

rely on 'matrix management' to save the day. The day will be over before the decision comes.

2 Big companies should have only five levels of management.

3 Put staff out in the field.

The new yardsticks support these prescriptions by mapping the business system and putting the focus on the operation as a whole and not on the individual functions or local agendas. One result of this horizontal focus is that some companies are establishing smaller work units, each with responsibility for a whole operation, a whole job, or a small but complete operating unit (e.g. store front area). A major benefit of cross-functional teams, and/or workcell base operations, is that fewer measures are needed. For example, in a furniture factory where one department makes the legs of a chair and another department assembles the chair, measures of performance would be reported to management by the leg fabrication department. In a workcell that has the equipment and capability to build the whole chair from start to finish, the workcell's performance as a whole would be measured and reported to management. The leg fabrication activity would be measured and managed within the workcell.

Support services such as purchasing, finance, and MIS are increasingly considered as being part of the workflow. Therefore, if they are integral to their customers' performance in the primary workflow, some organizations have decentralized these functions so that they are part of smaller, more autonomous work units. Again, there are fewer measures of department-to-department performance and more emphasis on work-unit-to-marketplace-customer performance.

Put the horse before the cart

For years, manufacturing has been both the battleground and source of competitive advantage. Statistical process control, JIT, activity accounting, and so on have helped manufacturers improve their processes, quality, and costs.

Today, the battle is moving upstream. Getting products that customers want into the marketplace quickly is the name of the game. Increasingly, companies are looking to gain competitive advantage by listening more attentively to customers' needs, designing more customized products to meet those demands, and delivering them to the marketplace in half the traditional development time.

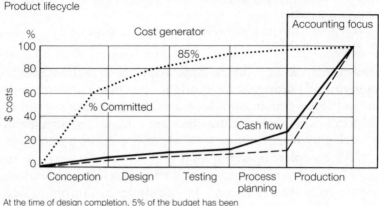

At the time of design completion, 5% of the budget has been spent, but 80% more is committed.

Figure 10.2   Product lifecycle costs
(adapted from Benjamin S. Blanchard, *Design and Manage to Life-Cycle Cost* (M/A Press, Portland, Oreg., 1978)

Similarly, more attention must be paid to the upstream costs committed during the new product introduction cycle. As figure 10.2 shows, 85 percent of the product's cost is committed in the new product introduction phase!

Many companies in Japan have been using a tool called 'target costing' to help reduce cost, not only in production but, more importantly, at the planning and design stage of the product lifecycle – before costs are committed.[6] Just as product and process designers must hit target values in terms of features, innovation, and performance, they must also be challenged to meet those design features within an allowable cost target – based on the cost drivers in the downstream departments (production and customer service). Some have argued that designers constrained by a cost target will be less innovative; forced to pick common parts, standard processes, etc. However, the experience of Japanese companies has been the opposite. By addressing trade-offs, they have been able to introduce more innovative products at a better price. Failure to address cost-planning issues early in the design phase can result in either innovative products that no one is willing to buy or cheap commodity products on the verge of extinction.

Empowering people to be master tailors

Performance does not change without people. As seen in case studies such as NUMMI, how human resources are nurtured, developed, and rewarded has more to do with world-class performance than computers and robots.

If people are your most valuable assets, treat them that way

Every employee in a company is a stakeholder in that company. Improvements in customer satisfaction, flexibility, and productivity will be achieved much more easily if every employee in the business system is involved. An involved workforce is an empowered workforce. When employees are given clear missions, challenging work, lots of responsibility, and appropriate feedback they become owners of their processes. Owners have vested interest in improvements. Just look at the volume of employee improvement suggestions in companies such as Canon and Honda. When thousands of ideas are implemented, this translates into formidable competition. Employee suggestions can be little things or breakthrough opportunities. For example, little things can mean a lot in the order fulfillment business system:

When Ford asked assembly line workers to contribute ideas for the new Ford Taurus, one employee suggested making all bolts the same size. Saving employees from sifting through bins of different size bolts and endlessly changing wrenches, makes the job go much faster. In another procedure, workers had to reach through a small hole in the car door to tighten a bolt. Employees worried that they would drop bolts inside the door, either slowing the assembly line to retrieve them or leaving behind a rattle for the future owner. The straightforward solution: enlarge the hole.[7]

But often, radical changes are required. When the Pacific rim countries began chipping away at Hewlett-Packard's workstation business, the company's Roseville terminal division had to do something dramatic. The general manager, Larry D. Mitchell, set the goal to beat the best:

Recognizing that the key was a design that could be put together easily, Mitchell abandoned the traditional phase review development cycle and teamed up engineers and specialists from marketing and manufacturing. The cross-functional teams designed a radically new terminal. It used 40% fewer parts than previous models and could be assembled in hours.[8]

Hewlett-Packard's product went from being a potential 'terminal' product line to being a trendsetter for the industry.

Companies employ people, not just their muscles. People who are challenged to do their best and use all their skills will be more productive. Furthermore, operations with whole people in them (doing many jobs: preventive maintenance, industrial engineering, quality control, etc.) also reduce the need for overhead.[9]

New roles for mid-level managers

Just as line workers learned new skills and multiple jobs in JIT workcells, managers and individual contributors must change with the times as well. While flatter organizations mean fewer managers, those managers will need new skills.

No doubt organizations will get flatter as competitive pressures mount on the vertical chains of command. General Electric has reduced nine levels to six. Wang Laboratories has similarly trimmed several levels of management. But what about the business system and department managers who survive? A new breed of manager will be found in the business operating system: one who is capable of maximizing the performance from cross-functional groups. Peter Drucker likens the job to conducting a symphony.[10] Perhaps Rosabeth Moss Kanter summarizes the impact best:

The old bases of managerial authority are eroding, and new tools of leadership are taking their place. Managers whose power derived from hierarchy and who were accustomed to a limited area of personal control are learning to shift their perspectives and widen their horizons. The new managerial work consists of looking outside a defined area of responsibility to sense opportunities and of forming project teams drawn from any relevant sphere to address them. It involves communications and collaboration across functions, across divisions, and across companies whose activities and resources overlap. Thus rank, title or official charter will be less important factors in success at the new managerial work than having the knowledge, skills, and sensitivity to mobilize people and motivate them to do their best.[11]

Staff and support organizations

A similar shock will hit corporate staff functions and support organizations. In many cases large corporate offices had about the same result as building high bay warehouses. Just as the factories became laden with inventory, corporate offices became layered with staffs that seemed to grow out of control. The curious thing about finished goods inventory in the warehouse and many staff functions is that they do not have customers.

Staff function exists to help the line people become more competitive. Plain and simple. As Cornell Maier, president of the Kaiser Aluminum and Chemical Corporation, once said: 'the only thing you really need to run a business are materials, machines, workers and salesmen. Nobody else is justified unless he's helping the worker produce more product or the salesman sell more product.' Staff and support functions should be close to their customers, the line operations. They are part of the BOS and should be measured accordingly.[12] Many companies have already begun moving staff functions directly into the value-added chain. For example, Westinghouse Electric has shifted staff functions, such as marketing, human resources, and communications, from the 'corporate towers' to specific business units. As John H. Maurer, senior consultant of Westinghouse's Productivity and Quality Center, puts it, there are two ways to streamline staff structures:

The most typical is surgery by ax and chain saw . . . In forcing arbitrary reductions in headcount, the processes supposedly are then forced into compliance. But when you examine it at a micro level, it can really create havoc – and have a crippling effect. Quality and customer satisfaction can be damaged . . . And you no longer have the people around who can fix it. Streamlining the process first, then adjusting the structure . . . is the right order.[13]

Communication

As organizations are reshaped and streamlined, communication patterns will change. As cycle times speed up, information will be more frequent. Also, as operations form tighter bonds around the horizontal business systems, communications flow two ways: back and forth between BOS leader and individuals within the BOS, and laterally between supplier and customer.

All employees should focus on improving their quality and delivery performance to their customer, while reducing their cycle time and eliminating waste. It is equally important that individuals identify with the BOS and understand how their work contributes to the success or failure of the business. Such identification can be achieved through reporting. The quality and delivery performance of each department should be made highly visible through the use of charts, operating meetings (with internal customers present), and scorecards. The quality and delivery performance of the entire business system should also be prominent in each department.

But scorecards alone will not be enough. Employees must share in the rewards of cross-functional improvement efforts.

Renovating the compensation system

One system that certainly must be mended in the new cross-functional, holistic-minded organization is the compensation and incentive system. As we have suggested, all employees in the business system need to feel ownership of the output of the business system as well as of its overall productivity. The performance measurement system we have designed focuses first on the success of the broader business system in delivering value to the customer. Local priorities and concerns take a distant second place. For example, an upstream department should willingly exceed its budget if it lowers overall cost in the entire business system. Yet all too often, compensation systems have built-in performance breakers such as 'performance to budget' measures as part of a department manager's review. Similarly individual workers may be motivated to keep machine utilization rates high as a measure of their productivity, regardless of whether their downstream user needs the extra output. To compensate for these shortcomings many companies are implementing various forms of gainsharing, in which all employees in an improvement effort share in the economic gains – regardless of the organization's boundaries.

Gainsharing

An increasing number of companies have implemented some form of gainsharing. Essentially gainsharing is an incentive program to promote and reward organization-wide teamwork.[14] Gainsharing plans have two components: an employee input channel (suggestions for improvement) and a bonus formula that tracks performance against operational objectives, calculates the impact of the improvement, and distributes cash bonuses among all organizational members. Several popular gainsharing formulas are Scanlon, Rucker, and Improshare.[15] Profit sharing is different from gainsharing in that it is linked to corporate conditions beyond an employee's control (e.g. tax provisions, pricing, market conditions, etc.).

Gainsharing rewards all workers in a particular business system for specific improvements within their control. For example: the Mead Corporation rewards plant workers equally for reaching specific goals in productivity, safety, and product quality;[16] Analog Devices similarly rewards all plant employees for meeting their Quality Improvement Plan goals. Gainsharing is a powerful tool to reinforce cross-functional teamwork. It is critical, therefore, that the right performance measures are used.

A new performance measurement system will be less effective without a new incentive system. A new incentive system could be a disaster if the wrong measures were rewarded. The two programs must go hand in glove.

Some resistance to gainsharing is surfacing in the union rank and file. For example, Boeing's 1989 strike slogan 'Dump the lump' refers to the union's preference for general wage increases over lump sum bonuses based on group performance. It is somewhat ironic that the first gainsharing plan was named after Joseph Scanlon, a union president in the 1930s. Scanlon developed the plan which bears his name in response to worker requests to help save their plant from closing![17]

Keeping the organization up to date

The concepts touched on briefly in this chapter suggest radically new ways of looking at the organization and how to behave in it. This kind of learning, for the most part, is not taught in business schools. Accounting courses have changed little since the 1950s. Organization Theory texts still portray the old, 'Eiffel Tower' organizational charts. Schools still graduate people to fill functional, limited jobs.

Organizations and the people within them will have to learn in new ways. As one CEO put it: 'The rate at which individuals and organizations learn may become the only sustainable competitive advantage, especially in knowledge-intensive industries.'[18] Just as group performance measurement differs from performance appraisal, organizational learning is different from individual learning. Individual learning happens when new knowledge and insights modify one person's behavior. Organizational learning occurs through shared insights, knowledge, and mental models. Therefore, organizations can only learn as quickly as the slowest link learns. Change is blocked unless all of the major decision-makers learn together, come to share beliefs and common goals, and are committed to take action.[19]

New performance measurement systems constitute one management tool that can accelerate organizational learning and build a consensus for change.

Summary

Management and employees can gain better control of their company's future by implementing a strategically driven, customer-focused performance measurement system that extends down to the department level. The operational acceptance and total impact can be enhanced by mending, altering, and remodeling related systems.

- The accounting system – because top-level financial reports are built upon accounting data. Therefore they need to be better synchronized with the operating measures.
- Return-on-investment equation – to capture the real benefits of technology, companies must measure the impact of new investments on the entire business system, using the criteria of improved quality and delivery, and reduced cycle time and waste.
- Information systems – only after the information environment is sanitized, simplified, and integrated, should companies seek to automate. Information should be stacked (related) so that managers can call up the information necessary for them to be able to take corrective action. All decision-makers need access to the data within their control.
- Organization design – as a cross-functional, outside-in view of the organization takes hold, it supplants the underlying logic of viewing organizations as a collection of separate functions.
- Human resources – if people are your most valuable assets, treat them that way. Every employee in a company is a stakeholder in that company. Improvements in customer satisfaction, flexibility, and productivity will be achieved much more easily if every employee in the business system is involved.
- Compensation – incentive programs promote and reward organization-wide teamwork. Gainsharing is a powerful tool to

reinforce cross-functional teamwork. It is critical, therefore, that the right performance measures are used.

Notes

1 We would like to thank Lou F. Jones, Cost and Business Analysis Manager at Caterpillar, for sharing with us Caterpillar's innovative approach to investment justification.
2 An excellent source of information on ESS can be found in John F. Rockart and David W. Delong, *Executive Support Systems* (Dow Jones/Irwin, Homewood, Ill., 1988).
3 Ray Stata, 'Organizational Learning – The Key to Management Innovation,' *Sloan Management Review*, Spring 1989.
4 Laurence M. Miller, *Barbarians to Bureaucrats* (Clarkson N. Potter Inc., New York, 1989).
5 Tom Peters, *Thriving on Chaos* (Harper & Row, New York, 1988).
6 Michiharu Sakurai, 'Target Costing and How to Use It,' *Journal of Cost Management*, Summer 1989.
7 James B. Treece, 'How to Teach Old Plants New Tricks,' *Business Week*, October–November 1989.
8 Jonathan B. Levine, 'How HP Built a Better Terminal,' *Business Week*, March 7, 1988.
9 Jeffrey G. Miller, Alfred J. Nanni, and Thomas E. Vollmann, 'Rethinking the Manufacturing Equations With Just-In-Time' (Boston University Manufacturing Roundtable, 1987).
10 Peter F. Drucker, 'The Coming of the New Organization,' *Harvard Business Review*, January–February 1988.
11 Rosabeth Moss Kanter, 'The New Managerial Work,' *Harvard Business Review*, November–December 1989.
12 Pacesetter Software, located in Princeton, New Jersey, has developed a nifty PC tool called 'Quality Map' that helps white-collar workers develop effective performance measures. The 'map' leads internal support functions through a process that includes painting the big picture (i.e. understanding the priorities of the broader business system(s) that the function supports), identifying the function's customers, defining the function's key services, and measuring the performance criteria that count to the customer.
13 John H. Sheridan, 'Sizing Up Corporate Staffs,' *Industry Week*, November 21, 1988.
14 Charles W. DeBettignies, 'Improving Organization-Wide Teamwork through Gainsharing,' *National Productivity Review*, vol. 8, no. 3, Summer 1989.

15 For an excellent review of these gainsharing programs and advice on how to choose the right approach for your company, see: Joseph H. Boyett and Henry Conn, *Maximum Performance Management: How to Manage and Compensate People to Meet World Class Competition* (Glenbridge, Macomb, Ill., 1988).

16 Shelley Liles-Morris, 'Battle of the Bonus,' *USA Today*, November 7, 1989.

17 DeBettignies, 'Improving Organization-Wide Teamwork.'

18 Stata, 'Organizational Learning.'

19 Ibid.

Conclusions

♦

B ritish statesman David Lloyd George once said that you cannot cross a chasm in two small jumps. He correctly observed that the wider the gap, the more imperative it becomes to take a quantum leap. Companies undergoing painful restructuring (a polite word for lay-offs) have learned that incremental improvements – judged by the old yardsticks – will fall short with disastrous consequences. Look what has happened to companies such as Kodak (lay-offs), Wang Laboratories (lay-offs), and Consumer Electronics (out of business). Reading the business papers is about as much fun as reading the obituaries!

Those who successfully jump the performance chasm will have learned how to compete on three critical dimensions of performance: customer satisfaction, flexibility, and productivity. The good news is that radical changes are already underway in many companies. The bad news is that most yardsticks in those same companies represent obstacles to change rather than aids to help organizations and the people in them learn faster.

From our discussions with hundreds of managers from a broad spectrum of industries in the United States and Europe, it is clear that changing the yardsticks will represent radical changes in what gets measured, who develops the measures, where measures are put in place, and how measures are used. The approach in this book builds upon several proven, world-class principles: total quality management, strategic planning, activity accounting, JIT, continuous improvement, and workflow simplification. We have integrated these principles into a consistent performance measurement system that reinforces doing the right things, and doing them well.

As any athlete knows, ability, the right equipment, and a desire to win are all important. Equally as important is the training program.

Below are ten 'training tips' to help you leap over the performance chasm.

Your stakeholders are rooting for you.

Ten ways to help your company measure up

Getting in shape

1 *Use performance measures to motivate behavior leading to continuous improvement.*
  Don't expect continuous improvement if performance measures are used just to whack people over the head. Employees are major stakeholders in the company. They want to do the right things, and do them well.

2 *Clearly communicate company and business strategies to everybody in the organization.*
  Without a strategy you do not know who your customers are. If you do not know who your customers are, how can you meet their expectations?

3 *Insist that the marketplace customer be the starting-point for how measures are developed.*
  Top-down, functionally driven measures tend to reflect an inside-out view of the world. Your customer is the future of your business. Develop measures from an outside-in perspective. Never lose sight of your customer.

On the practice field

4 *Draw a map of the workflow in your company's key business systems and focus on the supplier–customer networks that get the work done.*
  Mapping is a critical tool – and leads to streamlined operations that deliver better value to the customer.

5 *Shift the focus of the organization from being a bureaucratic, vertical empire to being a more responsive, horizontal business system.*
  Encourage the improved performance of the whole business system over that of any individual part. Think cross-functional. Better yet, act as a team.

6 *Listen to your customers and continually strive to meet their expectations of quality and delivery.*
  Customer satisfaction is not an 'intangible' that cannot be quantified. Customers will tell you what is important to them. Always put on the

customer's hat when measuring quality and delivery. If something does not make sense to them, how will it improve their satisfaction?

7 *Measure cycle times and waste within your control.*
Forget about the way you used to think about and measure productivity and cost. Reducing cycle times and eliminating waste are the keys to the productivity paradox.

On your marks, get set, go

8 *Measure the right stuff.*
Do not look for an off-the-shelf software solution or rely on some corporate guru to do it. Empower people to change the yardsticks by custom tailoring measures based on the needs of their customers and business strategies.

9 *Use a consistent, simple scorecard.*
There are no right number of measures for any organization or individual. But there are guidelines. There should be at least four (one each for quality, delivery, cycle time, and waste) but probably fewer than ten. Measures should be understandable at a glance, therefore avoid complex ratios and formulas. Graphs are better than numbers because they show movement over time. Measures should reinforce continuous improvement and lead to corrective action when performance does not meet expectations.

Keeping fit

10 *Use performance measures to accelerate organizational learning and build a consensus for change.*
Keep your measurement responsive to changes in customer expectations. The closer you are to the customer, the faster you can turn expectations into operational imperatives in the business system. Be sure to avoid confusion and conflicting signals. Do not let the accounting system or incentive system trip you up. With the proper mending and remodeling, they can give you the extra push to cross the chasm successfully.

Everyone wins with a consistent, well-focused measurement system. Customers are more consistently satisfied. Senior executives are more secure that their strategy is on track. Operating managers are focusing consistently on key result areas. This all adds up to better corporate performance for the stockholder and a more satisfying work environment for all employees.

Appendix A

◇

Workflow Improvement Principles

◆

As described in chapter 4, mapping is useful for highlighting previously overlooked opportunities to improve the flow of work within the BOS. All too often, maps of the business look more like a maze than a simple path to the customer. Reviewing such maps makes it painfully obvious that the flow of work, while explainable in small pieces, makes no sense at all from an overall business point of view. A map of the flow of work can also provide the foundation for understanding opportunities to apply JIT concepts and related work improvement principles whether in manufacturing, administration areas, or service businesses.

The purpose of this appendix is to describe workflow improvement principles which can be applied to the BOS and enhance the cross-functional flow of work (see figure A.1). These principles are intended to suggest actions which can be taken at the BOS level and department level to help the BOS achieve a balanced and simultaneous improvement in customer satisfaction, flexibility, and productivity.

Principles

The following principles, adapted from the works of Goldratt and Fox (1986) and Schonberger (1982), were initially designed for improving manufacturing operations.[1] (See additional reading at the end of Appendix A.) However, they have the same benefit in administrative operations as well!

1 *Establish a whole-product orientation* Activities related to the flow of

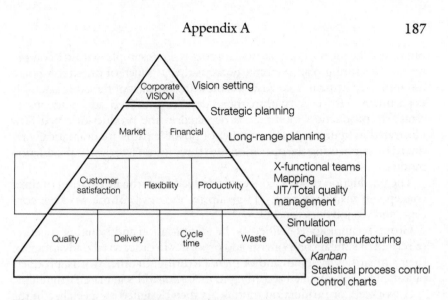

Figure A.1   The performance pyramid and a hierarchy of techniques

work can be organized by process or by product. In a process-oriented department each step of the process is consolidated, usually as a work center. For instance, all of the cutting machines are grouped together as a work center, feeding all of the drilling machines in a subsequent work center. The underlying principle is the maximization of equipment utilization. Unfortunately, this is accomplished at the expense of throughput time.

An effective alternative is to establish a product-oriented flow (see figure A.2). 'Product' does not necessarily mean the end product of the company,

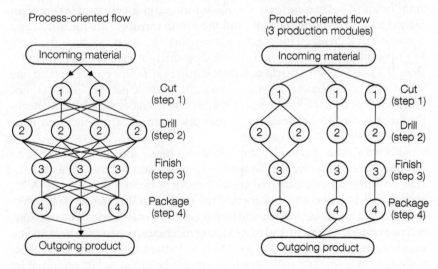

Figure A.2   Process versus product orientation

but rather the product of a particular process. For example, within a computer manufacturing plan, a circuit board is the 'product' of the circuit board
assembly department. Likewise, a cable is the product of the cable assembly
department. However, within those departments it is advantageous to
establish 'production modules' as depicted in the product-oriented flow
illustrated in figure A.2. The number of possible paths are dramatically reduced by segmenting the operation into three mini-factories, or production
modules.

The production module concept is derived from the integration of three
concepts in manufacturing: (1) group technology; (2) the workcell concept; and (3) job enrichment.

Group technology is defined as the identification and bringing together
of related or similar components and processes in order to take advantage of
their similarities in design and/or manufacturing. In other words, products
or assemblies are classified according to their similarities in manufacturability.

A workcell, or production module, is then designed to specialize in the
production of a particular family of products or assemblies. This specialization provides a product focus and enhances the capability to respond to
product revisions and new products. Product changes are facilitated by the
ability to communicate easily within a small group. Also, new product introduction problems and other changes only affect one group and not the
entire operation, as in a process-oriented layout. This greatly simplifies the
design and implementation of performance measures. Rather than measure
how well a portion of the process works, the process as a whole can be
measured.

The production module establishes a job design that is desirable from the
standpoint of human factors. A semi-autonomous group of workers is as-
signed to a production module, and the group members are measured and
rewarded as a group. This creates a teamwork situation in which the team
is responsible and accountable for its production quality and quantity.
People's jobs become enriched as they acquire proficiency at more than one
job and thereby become capable of building a whole piece or product, not
just a small portion of it. The result is that there is a more tangible and meaningful relationship between their work and both their product and their
product's impact on the company.

Although these principles are becoming more and more prevalent in
manufacturing they can also be applied to administrative workflow. For instance, in the process-oriented versus product-oriented flow (figure A.2),
step 1 could be opening and sorting the mail; step 2 could be data entry;
step 3 could be billing clerks; and step 4 could be mail clerks. The only difference would be that instead of grouping machines, the emphasis would be
on grouping people into small work teams. In the case of billing and collec-
tions for example, the small work teams might be organized by region or by
type of customer being serviced or by industry group.

2 *Establish non-stop processing* It is advantageous to process work as expeditiously as possible. As discussed in this book, rapid processing and an emphasis on reducing cycle time plays a key role in competitive performance. For example, the advantages of reducing time-to-market were discussed in chapter 7.

The implication is that a new commandment is required in day-to-day operations: 'Once a unit of work is started don't stop working on it until it is finished.' At the department level, achieving this objective might dictate that work units be processed individually rather than in batches. For instance, assume (see figure A.3) that the first processing step receives 25 units that take 5 minutes each to process. (A unit could be product in a factory or paperwork in an office.) Assume the second step also requires 5 minutes per unit. If the units are processed as a batch of 25 at both steps (i.e. all 25 units are completed before they are sent to the next operation), it will take 250 minutes, or just over 4 hours, until the units reach step 3. Processing the units individually, the first unit would reach step 3 in 10 minutes, and all 25 units would reach step 3 in 130 minutes, or just over 2 hours. In other cases throughput time and overall responsiveness is slowed by the means used physically to move the product or information. Automated material handling systems are a good case in point. Many companies invest heavily in fancy conveyors, robots, and warehouse systems to store and retrieve the mountains of inventory in the plant. All too often the result is more inventory and longer throughput times.

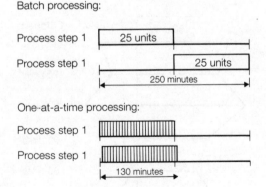

Figure A.3   Batch processing and one-at-a-time processing

The same problem occurs on the factory floor with the use of flow racks and conveyor systems for managing the work-in-process. Each movement of the product from one step to the next involves loading a tote bar of work from a work bench on to the conveyor, unloading the tote to the flow rack for storage. Later, when requested, the process continues with unloading the flow rack back to the conveyor, and unloading the conveyor on to the workbench. Even assuming that the load/unload and conveyance times are negligible, the fact that the product must be held means that time will be lost. A simple three-step, 20-minute operation, if hand-carried through the process, could easily take hours in actual throughput time.

However, if the operation were structured to allow a hand-off from one step to the next, throughput time would nearly equal the hands-on, value-added time. In addition, dramatic reductions in floor space and a reduction in confusion could be achieved. (It would also eliminate the need for sophis-ticated information systems to track the movement of work-in-process.)

3 *Balance the flow through the bottleneck*   Understanding the bottleneck, and balancing the flow through it, is one of the major optimized production technology (OPT) principles defined by Eliyahu Goldratt. It makes no sense to pass more material through any operation than the subsequent operation can handle.

For instance, figure A.4 displays a capacity to output 125 units per day at the first step. However, the fifth step can only handle 80 units per day. While every other step can handle more than 80 units, it is ineffective to do more than 80. Doing more than 80 will result in an accumulation of inventory prior to the fifth operation and, therefore, a reduction in throughput time. The output of the department as a whole is gated by the bottleneck, so the department is only capable of an 80 units per day output.

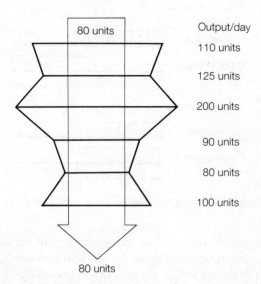

Figure A.4   Balance flow through the bottleneck

In real situations, bottlenecks are not usually fixed. They are typically dynamic, constantly changing in magnitude and location. The mix of product, the lot sizes, and the set-up times between lots all have a major impact on the bottleneck. The key is to be aware of the importance of the bottleneck and recognize that the process as a whole is regulated by it.

4 *Minimize sequential processing*   Sequential processing can create two problems that lengthen throughput time. First, the operations are dependent on each other and therefore gated by the slowest step. Second, no one person is responsible for the whole assembly or has a whole job.

Assume an assembly requires 20 minutes of labor to be put together (see figure A.5). In the sequential process, each individual gets one-quarter of the work, or 5 minutes per unit. But let us assume that the third person always takes 6 minutes per unit. It is irrelevant whether the reason is that he or she is slow or that the process is not properly balanced by engineering. In either case, the slowest step becomes the gate and limits production to 10 units per hour. In real situations the problem might not always be a particular person but rather a floating bottleneck created by fatigue, product, mix, etc. Sequential processing permits this kind of problem to occur.

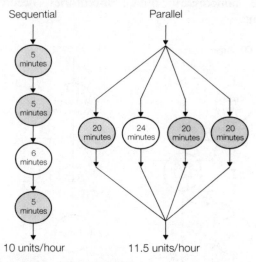

Figure A.5   Sequential and parallel processing

While sequential processing is an inevitable part of manufacturing, in many cases it is not essential. Sequential steps can at times be replaced with parallel processing. In the example, if each of the four people do the whole assembly, output per hour could be increased by 15 percent. The slowest person could still work at the same pace and take 20 percent more time, but this would not affect the others' productivity.

For some manufacturers, material preparation and/or kitting is a part of the manufacturing process that unnecessarily creates an additional sequential step. Often it is possible to store components at the work-bench and give the assembler the instructions to pick (and prepare) the parts as required.

From the standpoints of human factors and of quality, parallel processing is beneficial. Each worker can take pride in building a whole assembly and therefore will accept responsibility for productivity and quality. It then becomes possible to eliminate another sequential step: inspection.

Also, controlling the flow of work and its quality is difficult with many sequential and independent steps. For example, even if at each step everything goes right 99 percent of the time, in a 50-step sequential process the odds are that only 60 percent of the time will the entire process perform correctly. In order to depend on the process as a whole, each step must be designed to work correctly 100 percent of the time. One means of improving quality of process is to consolidate activities into fewer parallel steps.

5 *Minimize multiple paths through specialized operations*   Multiple paths create confusion and a balancing and scheduling nightmare. Buffer inventories are typically employed to relieve the symptoms, and bury the problem. Unfortunately, unnecessary buffer inventories needlessly add to throughput time.

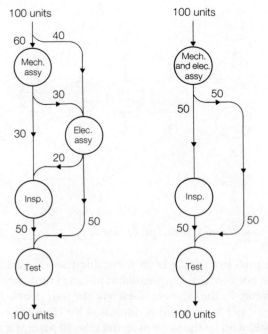

Figure A.6   Minimize multiple paths

In the illustration on the left in figure A.6, it is easy to see why inventories might be used to eliminate the complexity of scheduling and balancing. The operation depicted produces an electro-mechanical assembly with a mechanical assembler, an electrical assembler, an inspector, and a tester. The 100 units entering the operation do not all follow the same path. At the very beginning, there is a 60 : 40 split, with 40 of the 100 bypassing mechanical assembly. Those 40 units go to electrical assembly, along with 30 units from mechanical assembly. Subsequently, 50 units bypass inspection and go directly to test, while the other 50 go through inspection. In actual situations, the quantity or percentage of product that travels each route could change hourly.

The process on the right in figure A.6 does exactly the same job in a greatly simplified manner. The simplification is accomplished by using assemblers who are responsible for both mechanical and electrical assembly. Elimination of the distinction between mechanical and electrical assemblers immediately makes the process more manageable. There is only one bypass loop to be reckoned with. At the same time, jobs are enriched since each individual is given the whole assembly job. In many cases this would make it possible to eliminate inspection completely. It might also be possible to make each assembler responsible for his or her own testing.

Conclusion

In summary, significant improvements in competitive performance can be achieved by integrating the workflow principles into the design and management of day-to-day operations. These principles are:

1 Establish a whole-product orientation.
2 Establish non-stop processing.
3 Balance the flow through the bottleneck.
4 Minimize sequential processing.
5 Minimize multiple paths.

In addition, the creation of whole jobs has been recommended in connection with a number of these principles. That is because these principles are more easily achieved through this approach to job design. While these principles can be designed into the process, it is the workers who will make them effective. Their flexibility to handle multiple tasks and to contribute ideas as well as routine work can make possible dramatic improvements in competitive performance.

Note

1 Kelvin F. Cross, 'Making Manufacturing More Effective Through Reduced Throughput Time,' *National Productivity Review*, Winter 1986–7.

Additional Readings

Hiroyuki Hirano, ed., *JIT Factory Revolution: A Pictorial Guide to Factory Design of the Future* (Productivity Press, Cambridge, Mass., 1988).

Richard Schonberger, *Japanese Manufacturing Techniques: Nine Hidden Lessons in Simplicity* (Free Press, New York, 1982).

Eliyahu M. Goldratt and Robert E. Fox, *The Race – For a Competitive Advantage* (Creative Output, Conn., 1986).

Russell M. Barefield and S. Mark Young, *Internal Auditing in a Just-In-Time Environment* (Institute of Internal Auditors Research Foundation, Allamonte Springs, Fla, 1988).

Kelvin F. Cross and John Feather, 'Workflow Analysis, Just-In-Time Techniques Simplify Administrative Process in Paperwork Operation,' *Industrial Engineering*, January 1988.

Robert W. Hall, *Attaining Manufacturing Excellence* (Dow Jones/Irwin, Homewood, Ill., 1987).

Appendix B

◇

Enlightened measures

◆

Computer manufacturing company: business operating system for a new product introduction

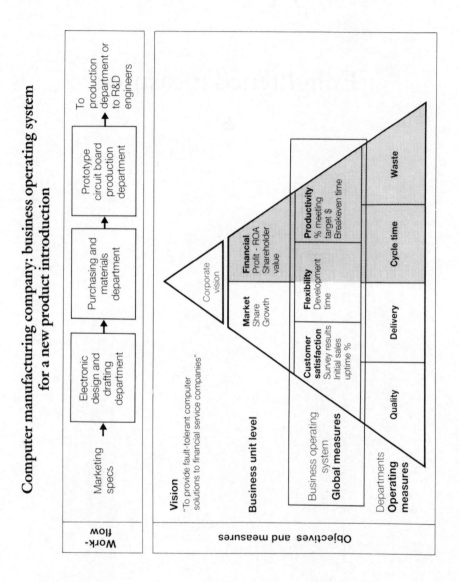

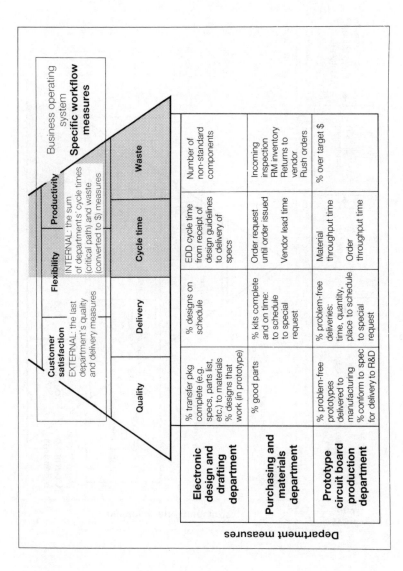

Department measures	Quality	Delivery	Cycle time	Waste
Electronic design and drafting department	% transfer pkg complete (e.g. specs, parts list, etc.) to materials % designs that work (in prototype)	% designs on schedule	EDD cycle time from receipt of design guidelines to delivery of specs	Number of non-standard components
Purchasing and materials department	% good parts	% kits complete and on time: to schedule to special request	Order request until order issued Vendor lead time	Incoming inspection RM inventory Returns to vendor Rush orders
Prototype circuit board production department	% problem-free prototypes delivered to manufacturing % conform to spec for delivery to R&D	% problem-free deliveries: time, quantity, place to schedule to special request	Material throughput time Order throughput time	% over target $

Business operating system
Specific workflow measures

Customer satisfaction EXTERNAL: the last department's quality and delivery measures	Flexibility	Productivity

INTERNAL: the sum of departments' cycle times (critical path) and waste (converted to $) measures

Computer manufacturing company: a section of the business operating system for order fulfillment

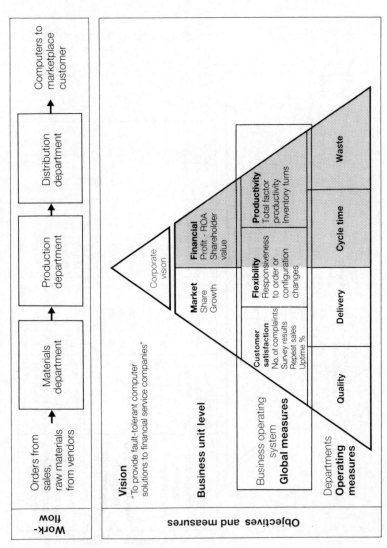

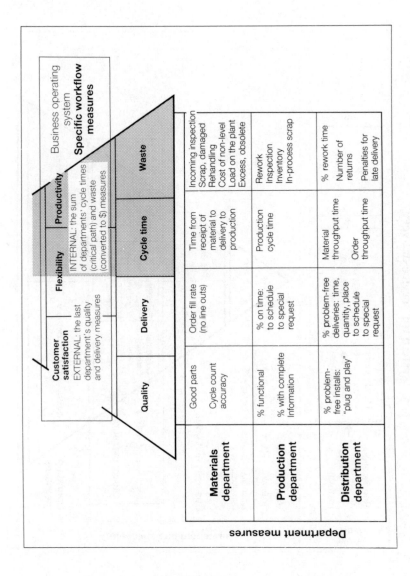

The following table represents the content within the figure:

	Customer satisfaction EXTERNAL: the last department's quality and delivery measures		Flexibility	Productivity INTERNAL: the sum of departments' cycle times (critical path) and waste (converted to $) measures	Business operating system Specific workflow measures
	Quality	Delivery		Cycle time	Waste
Materials department	Good parts Cycle count accuracy	Order fill rate (no line outs)		Time from receipt of material to delivery to production	Incoming inspection Scrap, damaged Rehandling Cost of non-level Load on the plant Excess, obsolete
Production department	% functional % with complete Information	% on time: to schedule to special request		Production cycle time	Rework Inspection Inventory In-process scrap
Distribution department	% problem-free installs: "plug and play"	% problem-free deliveries: time, quantity, place to schedule to special request		Material throughput time Order throughput time	% rework time Number of returns Penalties for late delivery

Department measures

Chain of fitness centers: a section of the business operating system for service delivery

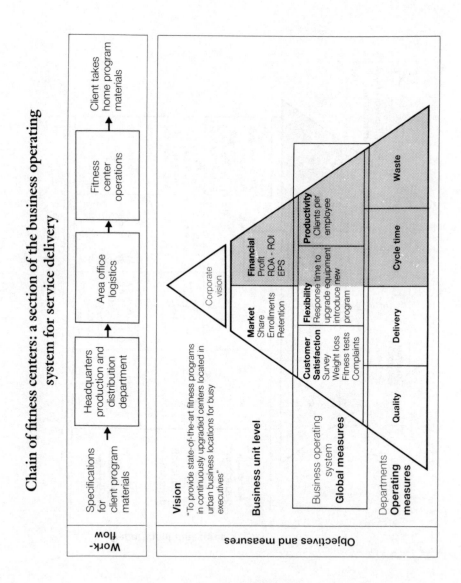

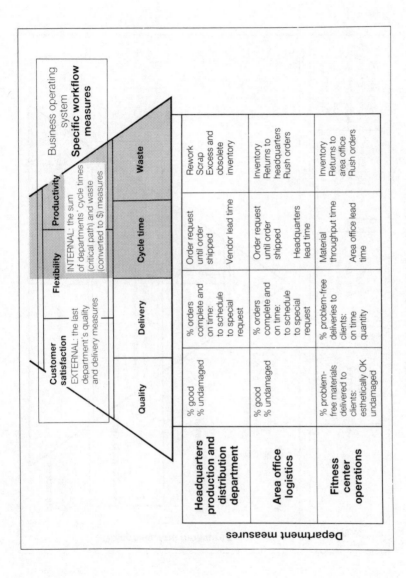

Business operating system — Specific workflow measures

	Customer satisfaction — EXTERNAL: the last department's quality and delivery measures		Flexibility	Productivity — INTERNAL: the sum of departments' cycle times (critical path) and waste (converted to $) measures	
Department measures	Quality	Delivery	Cycle time	Waste
Headquarters production and distribution department	% good % undamaged	% orders complete and on time: to schedule to special request	Order request until order shipped Vendor lead time	Rework Scrap Excess and obsolete inventory
Area office logistics	% good % undamaged	% orders complete and on time: to schedule to special request	Order request until order shipped Headquarters lead time	Inventory Returns to headquarters Rush orders
Fitness center operations	% problem-free materials delivered to clients: esthetically OK undamaged	% problem-free deliveries to clients: on time quantity	Material throughput time Area office lead time	Inventory Returns to area office Rush orders

Chain of fitness centers: a section of the business operating system for revenue management

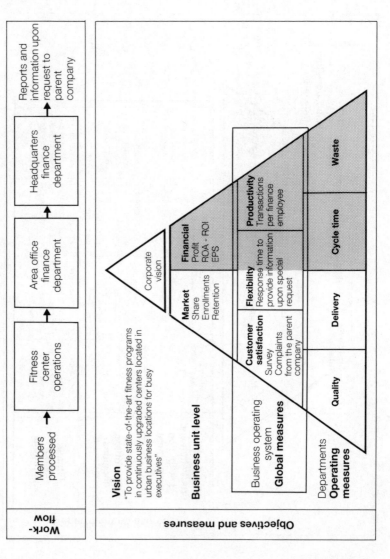

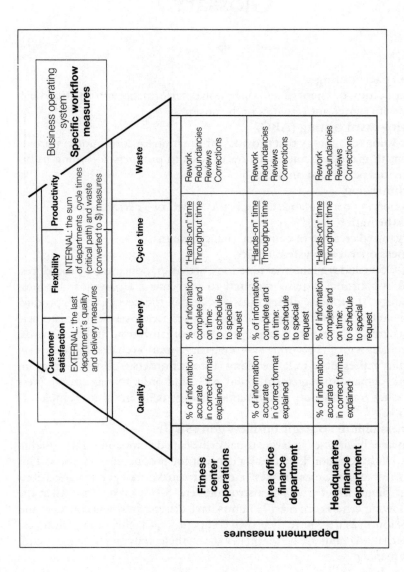

Business operating system **Specific workflow measures**				
Customer satisfaction EXTERNAL: the last department's quality and delivery measures		**Flexibility**	**Productivity** INTERNAL: the sum of departments cycle times (critical path) and waste (converted to $) measures	
Quality	**Delivery**	**Cycle time**	**Waste**	
Fitness center operations	% of information: accurate in correct format explained	% of information complete and on time: to schedule to special request	"Hands-on" time Throughput time	Rework Redundancies Reviews Corrections
Area office finance department	% of information accurate in correct format explained	% of information complete and on time: to schedule to special request	"Hands-on" time Throughput time	Rework Redundancies Reviews Corrections
Headquarters finance department	% of information accurate in correct format explained	% of information complete and on time: to schedule to special request	"Hands-on" time Throughput time	Rework Redundancies Reviews Corrections

Department measures

Glossary

◆

Activity accounting
A collection of financial and operational performance information dealing with significant activities of the business.

Activity-based costing (ABC)
A costing technology that provides information for continuous improvement in manufacturing. ABC traces costs to products according to the activities performed on them.

Benchmarking
Comparing performance to the best competitor's performance.

Breakthrough
Organized creation of beneficial change (Juran).

Business operating system (BOS)
A BOS includes all internal functions, activities, policies and procedures, and supporting systems required to implement a particular business strategy. It includes all functions involved in the development, production and provision of specific products or services to particular customers – wherever these may reside in the total organization. In other words, emphasis is given to workflow – not to organization charts. A production facility represents a BOS for filling customer orders (subsystems may include demand management, build cycle, and order management). New product introduction and revenue management are also examples of BOSs.

Business unit or strategic business unit (SBU)
Separate businesses in large, usually diversified companies. First used in the US by General Electric as a concept for product classification. This form of organization makes it easier to make independent decisions regarding market share, cost structure, etc. SBUs make sense when the following criteria are met: (1) units have distinct business concepts and missions; (2) they have their own competitors; (3) their competitors are external; (4) units are better off managing their strategies in an independent manner.

Control
Process of detecting and correcting adverse change (Juran).

Control chart
A statistical device usually for the study and control of repetitive processes. It is designed to reveal the randomness or trend of deviations from a mean or control value, usually by plotting the data.

Cost accounting
Techniques used for: proper inventory valuation based on generally accepted accounting practices; strategic information related to product line profitability, pricing and make-versus-buy; and performance measures for operational control.

Cost of quality
All costs (labor, materials, overhead) attributed to preventing non-conformance, appraising/checking output to ensure conformance to requirements, and correcting internal and external failures. Cost of quality is not a manufacturing term. It also refers to the quality of administrative workflows. For example, the salesperson who books an incorrect order, the clerk who has to make sure the order is clean and the rework of the order are all examples of costs of quality.

Cost/waste
The non-value-added activities and resources incurred in meeting the requirements of the customer. Waste includes all the costs associated with failures, appraisals, and surpluses.

Critical success factors (CSFs)
A term popularized by John Rockart of MIT's Sloan Management School based on his research in executive information needs. In his words, CSFs are 'those few critical areas where things must go right for the business to flourish.'

Customer
The customer in the marketplace. The reason your company exists. When services are involved (e.g. legal, consulting, etc.) the customer is called a client.

Customer satisfaction
How customer expectations regarding quality and delivery are managed in the BOS. High-quality products or services (based on customer-driven target values) and regular on-time delivery are the paths to customer satisfaction.

Cycle time
The sum of process time, move time, inspect time, queue time, and storage time. Only process time is considered 'value-added' time.

Decision support system (DSS)
An *integrated* management information and planning system that provides users with the ability to: (1) query databases and information systems; (2) analyze the information in various ways; and (3) predict the impact of decisions before they are made.

Delivery
The quantity of product or service delivered on time to the customer, user, next department, etc.

Department
Component of a business system.

Division

A set of quasi-autonomous entities linked together by a central administrative structure.

Executive information system (EIS)

An information system for managers that consolidates and summarizes ongoing transactions within the organization. An EIS should be able to provide management with all the information it requires at all times from external as well as internal sources.

Executive support system (ESS)

The routine use of a computer-based system, most often through direct access to a terminal or personal computer, for any business function. The users are either the CEO or a member of the senior management team reporting directly to him or her. Executive support systems can be implemented at the corporate or divisional level.

Flexibility

Addresses the responsiveness of the BOS. The combination of *externally* driven delivery (when the customer wants to take delivery of a product) and *internally* driven cycle time (how we can reduce the time to make a product) defines flexibility.

Gainsharing

An incentive program to promote and reward organization-wide teamwork. Gainsharing involves the entire organization in an improvement efforts and 'shares' the economic 'gains' with all members of the organization. Gainsharing plans have two components: an employee input channel (suggestions for improvement) and a bonus formula that tracks performance against operational objectives, calculates the impact of the improvement, and distributes cash bonuses to all organizational members.

Group

Multiples of divisions grouped by region or broad product divisions. For example, Hewlett-Packard has a workstation group with several divisions, such as the Apollo division.

Internal customer

Next operation, department or user downstream in the value-added chain. The reason your function or department exists.

Just-in-time (JIT)

A term coined by Westerners to describe what they observed in Japanese factories. Ironically, Taiichi Ohno, an engineer at Toyota, borrowed much of his JIT materials approach by observing US supermarkets, where clerks frequently replenished the shelves. In a very narrow sense, JIT refers to the movement or transport of material so as to have only the necessary material at the necessary place at the necessary time. In a broader sense, JIT is a system characterized by a commitment to continuous improvement in activities and the quality of products, while eliminating waste (including wasted time).

Management by objectives (MBO)

Originally a process in which manager and subordinate agree on individual job goals, which serve as the basis for personal performance assessment. Subsequent modifications expanded the scope to include a system for managing an organization by holding managers accountable, encouraging all employees to contribute to department goals, coordinating goals within the organization, and measuring results.

Management control system

A process by means of which managers ensure that resources are obtained and used effectively and efficiently in the accomplishment of the organization's objectives.

Mapping

Creating a type of flow chart which depicts the activities required to operate a portion of the business or all of the business. In essence, a 'business map' provides clear documentation as to the supplier–customer relationship throughout the business. A business map depicts how the business works by: (1) highlighting all contacts and activities with the end-user; (2) highlighting all contacts and activities with the distribution channel; and (3) highlighting the relationship between the backroom activities required to support the distribution channel and the end-user. This clear representation of activities ensures that both the end-user and the distribution channel contacts are visible and are considered in the development of performance measurements.

Operational control

The process of ensuring that specific tasks are carried out effectively and efficiently.

Pareto chart

A histogram showing the cumulative frequency of defects. It helps to focus on the top failures. Generally, 20 percent of the causes account for 80 percent of the defects.

Performance appraisal

Feedback on an individual's contribution to his or her department, usually done in conjunction with salary/wage review.

Performance measurement

Feedback on activities that motivate behavior leading to continuous improvement in customer satisfaction, flexibility, and productivity. It is *not* an employee evaluation.

Process control

The systematic evaluation of a process, and the taking of corrective action if performance fails to meet a standard.

Process time

Refers to the actual time it takes for a department to complete the work from the time the work is requested of the department, i.e. the throughput time. When used in the context of cycle time, it is the time an operation is adding value to the product or service.

Productivity

Refers to how resources (including time) are managed. Emphasis on waste reduction and faster process times improves productivity.

Quality

Consistent conformance to customer expectations, 100 percent of the time, through the delivery, defect-free, of product or service.

Quality assurance

All the planned or systematic actions necessary to provide adequate confidence that the product or service will satisfy the customer.

Quality control

Operational techniques and activities to sustain the quality of a product or service. A regulatory process to measure actual quality performance. (Compare with process control.)

Quality function deployment (QFD)

A system for designing products or services based on customer demands and involving all members of the producer/supplier organization.

Stakeholders

Those who have a stake in a company and how it performs: the customer, the stockholder, employees, suppliers, and the community.

Statistical process control

The use of statistics in conjunction with process control.

Strategic control system

System for linking operations to strategic goals, integrating financial and non-financial information to support internal business decisions, and focusing activities on customer requirements.

Strategic objectives

Actions or changes required in the organization stated in measurable terms.

Strategic planning

The process of deciding on the objectives of the organization, on changes in these objectives, on the resources used to attain these objectives, and on the policies that govern the acquisition, use, and disposition of these resources.

Target costing

A cost management tool for reducing the overall cost of a product over its entire lifecycle with the help of production, engineering, R&D, marketing, and accounting.

Total quality control (TQC)

An effective system for integrating the quality development, quality maintenance, and quality improvement efforts of the various groups in an organization so as to enable production and service at the most economical levels which allow for full customer satisfaction.

Vendor scheduling

A purchasing approach which provides vendors with schedules rather than individual hard copy purchase orders.

Waste

The non-value-added activities and resources incurred in meeting the requirements of the customer. Waste includes all the costs associated with failures, appraisals, and surpluses. Pure waste consists of those activities and related expenses that are totally unnecessary, such as scrap and rework. Hidden waste comprises those costs associated with activities that do not add value, such as inspection and storage. These wasteful activities are typically necessary because of existing operating conditions and strategies.

Workcell

A grouping of machines and people to perform a set of tasks.

Index